THE
Wholesome Baby Food
GUIDE

THE
Wholesome Baby Food
GUIDE

Over 150 Easy, Delicious, and Healthy
Recipes from Purees to Solids

MAGGIE MEADE

GRAND CENTRAL
Life & Style

NEW YORK · BOSTON

Grand Central Life & Style
Hachette Book Group
237 Park Avenue
New York, NY 10017

www.HachetteBookGroup.com

Printed in the United States of America

Binder's code: RRD-C

First Edition: February 2012
10 9 8 7 6 5 4 3 2 1

Grand Central Life & Style is an imprint of Grand Central Publishing. The Grand Central Life & Style name and logo are trademarks of Hachette Book Group, Inc.

The publisher is not responsible for websites (or their content) that are not owned by the publisher.

Library of Congress Cataloging-in-Publication Data
Meade, Maggie.
The wholesome baby food guide : 150 easy, delicious, and healthy recipes from purees to solids / Maggie Meade.
—1st ed.
p. cm.
ISBN 978-0-446-58410-4
1. Baby foods.   2. Infants—Nutrition.   I. Title.
TX740.M368 2012
641.5'6222—dc23
2011022441

This book is dedicated to Nick and John and Jake, my three sons and taste testers, who continue to teach and inspire me daily with their love and presence; to John, husband and partner who humors and loves me through thick and thin, messy kitchens and purees, finger foods, and table foods, too. And to all parents who dare to step into the kitchen and make their babies' food, giving their babies the gift of fresh flavors and real tastes, I applaud and dedicate this to you.

ACKNOWLEDGMENTS

With unending gratitude, I would like to first thank all the Wholesome Baby Food website visitors who over the past eight years have shared with me their praise, criticism, encouragement, and enthusiasm, which continue to inspire and humble me: this book is for all of you. Thank you to "Gramma Jay Jay" and "Poppy" Dextraze, whose love and support have saved me and carried me through good times and bad; to Diana Baroni, my editor at Grand Central, who believed that this book could indeed transcend the website and who hung in there during times of turbulence; to Naomi Rosenberg and Andrew Rosen, two of the finest pediatricians I have been fortunate to know and have as physicians. They approach their patients with open hearts, open minds, and open ears, knowing that good health is not just about medicine. Thank you to Kris Howe, Melina Gosselin, Nancy O'Leary, and Jenn Driscoll, who long ago at a play date thought I should create a website, and to Tracy Lawman, who may have grown tired of hearing about my writing but continued to support me and meet me for Friday coffee.

CONTENTS

PART II
Homemade Baby Food—Recipes and Tips for Feeding Your Baby with Wholesome Goodness and Love!   97

STAGE THREE: Eight Months of Age and Older—Adventurous Foods for Budding Foodies

FRUITS

VEGETABLES

INTRODUCTION

Since you have picked up this book, you likely have a baby who is about to begin eating solid foods or you know someone who does. *The Wholesome Baby Food Guide* is perfect for anyone who wants to know more about how to introduce solid foods, the various stages of solid foods, and infant nutrition. Within these pages you will find no-nonsense, straightforward information and recipes. I know that parents today don't have a lot of time to waste slogging through medical jargon or creating fancy recipes with ingredients that are hard to find at the local grocery store. You see, I am not a trained chef or a pediatrician, but I do have a passion for empowering parents to trust their instincts and their cooking abilities. When I set out to write this book, my goal was to help my readers gain confidence in themselves, to realize that it's not necessary to be medically trained or have a certificate from a culinary institution to be able to provide the best nutrition possible for their little ones.

In 2003, I began writing and publishing the Wholesome Baby Food website, which over the years has become a trusted resource for parents to learn about solid foods and feeding babies. This book combines the best of the website, with lots of familiar ideas and recipes, along with new content and recipes found only within these pages. It has been a wonderful experience writing this book so that parents everywhere will be able to learn about baby food stages and whip up fresh and easy homemade baby food, beginning healthy eating habits right from the start. I am also delighted to be able to fulfill the requests of many of the website's visitors and offer up a "real" book they can hold in their hands and take into the kitchen. Now go forth and puree!

PART I

The Journey into
Solid Foods

Of all the milestones a baby will reach in the first year, beginning solid foods is one of the most nerve-racking and confusing (not to mention messy). As a parent, you will likely be bombarded with "friendly" but maddeningly conflicting advice offered by well-intentioned friends and family. I can still recall all the confusing advice I received about feeding my own babies. (With my twins, a few people even suggested that I let one twin be the "taste tester" to determine what foods I should eventually feed them both. Looking back, I wonder if this might be the reason John always lets his brother try new foods first. Did the boys overhear this advice when they were still in their infant carriers and decide between the two of them who should go first?) Once you get past the myths and the folklore, starting your baby on solid foods does not have to be scary. Armed with the right information and a good sense of humor, you will find that introducing solids can be a fun adventure for you both.

CHAPTER ONE

A Discussion of Introducing Solid Foods at Each Stage

As you contemplate starting your baby on solid foods, it's important to note what various medical organizations recommend. The American Academy of Pediatrics (AAP), along with many other health agencies such as the World Health Organization and UNICEF, states that breast milk and/or formula should provide all the nutrition your baby needs during the first six months of life. However, the AAP Committee on Nutrition also notes that introducing solid foods between four and six months is perfectly acceptable; introducing babies to solids prior to four months is not recommended. Regardless of whether you start at four, five, or six months, or even later, keep in mind that solid foods will not make up a large portion of your baby's nutrition for quite a few weeks after you start. Remember that you are *introducing* your baby to solid foods, not suddenly changing your baby's diet. At this point, the term *complementary foods* is often used instead of *solid foods*, and this term best describes the early role of solids. In the beginning, you are complementing breast milk and/or formula with solid foods, not replacing them. The first few weeks should be a time to take it slow, keep it simple, and stay relaxed. Explore and enjoy the experience of watching your baby touch and taste his or her way through the wonderful world of food!

How will I know when my baby is ready to eat solid foods?

When a baby hits three or four months of age, many parents start to feel that he or she may need "something more" than formula or breast milk. Your baby may suddenly be waking up more often at night or eating more often than has been typical. But it's important to remember that while waking at night for a feeding *could* indicate that your baby is ready for solid food, there might be another reason: the growth spurt that typically occurs between three and four months of age. This growth spurt often accounts for your baby's increased appetite but is not necessarily a sign that your baby needs solid foods. You see, babies have a tremendous ability to know just what they need and when they need it. These demands for increased feedings are your baby's way of obtaining the crucial nutrition his or her body needs during this time of rapid growth. Remember, during these early months, formula and/or breast milk are your baby's most important source of nutrition.

Studies show that babies are highly individual in developing a readiness for solid foods. One baby might seem to be ready at four months, while another shows no signs of readiness until around six or seven months. Since appetite alone is not a reliable indication, here are a few key signs to look for when trying to determine if your baby is ready to begin the journey into solid foods:

- *Has baby lost the tongue thrust reflex?* In the first four months, the tongue thrust reflex prevents a baby from choking on foreign objects. When any unusual substance is placed on the tongue, it automatically protrudes outward rather than back. Between four and six months of age, this reflex gradually diminishes. Until the reflex is gone, solid foods won't have a chance of making it into baby's belly.
- *Has baby developed the ability to signal that she is full?* Your baby will develop the ability to let you know that she is full from a "meal" with signs such as turning away from the bottle or breast and/or clamping her mouth shut. This signaling ability is critical for allowing her to regulate the amount of food she is eating and helps her avoid overeating.
- *Is baby able to sit up and hold his head up unassisted?* This milestone is important because babies who must be reclined to be fed are at greater risk of choking. Also, the ability to sit up and have head control has long been associated with the physical maturity that might indicate baby is ready to eat solids. Most pediatricians are in agreement that this milestone is a clear indicator that a baby is ready to begin solid foods.
- *Has baby's birth weight doubled?* The doubling of birth weight is a rough rule of thumb that baby is ready for solid foods. It's far from an exact rule, though, so you should consider the other signs as well.

Some infant developments that are traditionally viewed as a sign of readiness for solid foods are less reliable:

- *Interest in your food.* This could signal a readiness for food but it may not be the best sign: when a baby reaches four to six months of age, he is interested in putting everything in his mouth!

- *Frequently waking in the middle of the night when a consistent sleeping pattern had been established.* As noted earlier, although frequent waking could be a sign of readiness for solids, it's not a reliable sign. Baby may be waking (and nursing/feeding) for any number of reasons: illness, teething, or even a growth spurt. Unfortunately, as you will learn over the coming months and years, sleeping patterns are often disrupted for all sorts of reasons even long after your child is on a solid food diet.

Watch Your Baby, Not the Calendar

As you know, all babies are different individuals. Don't worry if your baby does not take to solid foods "on schedule," and don't let others try to convince you that your three-month-old looks hungry and needs to eat some cereal. Pay attention to your baby's signals and cues, and "watch your baby, not the calendar" when thinking about starting solids. Most important, don't let others make you feel guilty or second-guess your decisions. You know your baby best! Don't be pushed into starting solids early, and don't ever feel you are a "bad" parent if you believe your baby is or is not ready for solids before he or she is six months old.

Discuss the pros and cons of introducing solid foods with your pediatrician—and don't be afraid to voice your own views and concerns. If your pediatrician insists that you start your four-month-old infant on solids and you don't feel your baby is ready, voice your concerns and ask the pediatrician to explain his or her recommendation. The ensuing discussion might surprise you and help you make a decision.

My Parent/Grandma/Sister et al.
Insist That My Two- or Three-Month-Old
Baby Needs "Real Food"

Some parents may be tempted to give in to relatives, grandmothers, friends, and sometimes even their own mothers, who may say things like "Give that baby some real food, she's starving" or "Nursing that baby isn't enough, he needs some real food." Remember that breast milk and/or formula is "real food." These contain all the important nutrients an infant needs to develop properly. In fact, introducing solids too early may displace the important nutrition your baby needs to receive from breast milk and/or formula. Your baby needs formula/breast milk first; solid foods will not offer the proper balance or amount of nutrients to sustain healthy growth.

Is it ever too late to introduce solid foods to a baby?

There are two reasons babies can indeed be introduced to solids "too late" (the term *late* here means later than six months of age):

- *Allergies.* Since 2007, several clinical studies have pointed to the possibility that the late introduction of solid foods might increase the risk of allergies both to foods and to airborne substances such as pollen. While research in this area is not yet conclusive, risking an allergy to certain foods is one reason not to wait longer than approximately six months of age to introduce solids.

- *Iron Requirements.* Babies are born with iron stored in their bodies. Around six (and some say up to eight) months of age, these iron stores will become gradually depleted and leave your baby at risk for iron-deficient anemia. While your baby's iron will not disappear completely, her levels may fall significantly. So waiting too long to introduce solid foods may put her at risk for anemia.

You may have heard that there is a "window of opportunity" for a baby to learn how to chew and eat solid foods. This is more myth than fact. There is *no* evidence that babies who are started relatively late on solids have any trouble learning to chew and swallow. When your baby is ready, he will eat! If a baby has reached the age of seven to eight months and continues to have no interest in eating solid foods, you should consult with your pediatrician, as there may be developmental or other issues going on.

My baby is ready to eat solid foods; how should I start and what should I feed?

There are a few things to keep in mind as you begin the transition to solid foods. Two of the most important are to (1) take it slow; and (2) keep it simple. Choosing which food to start your baby on is one of the fun aspects of beginning solid foods. Here are a few great choices for nutritious and tasty starter foods for your baby.

First Foods
Why These Are Good Choices

Fruits

avocados, bananas, pears, apples	Smooth, creamy, and lightly sweet, these fruits are loaded with important nutrients, and they are also easily digested.

Vegetables

sweet potatoes, acorn or butternut squash, green beans	Orange vegetables like sweet potatoes and squash are really tasty; they can be made smooth and creamy, and they're packed full of vitamin A, vitamin C, and even some iron. Green beans also make a great first food for those who wish to start with vegetables that are green.*

Grains

rice, oats	Rice and oats are two traditional starter grains for babies. They are not highly allergenic and are relatively easy to digest. Brown rice and steel-cut oats may be easily made into "baby cereal" and offer the most nutrients.

---

*While research shows that babies (and humans of all ages) are born with an innate preference for sweet tastes, many pediatricians still recommend offering green vegetables first and fruits second to encourage a taste for foods that are less sweet.

Isn't rice cereal always the first food?

As you can see, there are many nutritious food options for your baby's first food besides rice cereal. While rice cereal has been the traditional first food, there is no reason that you absolutely must start solid foods with rice. Many pediatric resources are starting to acknowledge that avocado, banana, and sweet potato make great first foods for babies. The AAP now states, "For most babies it does not matter what the first solid foods are. By tradition, single-grain cereals are usually introduced first. However, there is no medical evidence that introducing solid foods in any particular order has an advantage for your baby." Rice cereal can be a good starter food because it is low on the allergen list, is relatively easy to digest, and provides additional iron. However, skipping the cereal and starting with a tastier fruit or vegetable might be perfect for your baby. In a 2009 interview with *Pediatric News*, Dr. Frank Greer, of the Committee on Nutrition at the American Academy of Pediatrics, indicated that solid foods for babies should be introduced based on their nutritional makeup and not on simple tradition. In fact, offering rice cereal as a first food does not make a lot of sense because it is low in protein and high in carbohydrates.

Is there a risk of iron-deficiency anemia if fortified rice cereal is skipped?

As solid foods are introduced, parents often worry that their baby is not getting enough iron. Rest assured, the vast majority of babies will not become iron-deficient if they do not eat a fortified baby rice cereal, nor will they become iron-deficient if they do not receive supplements. Even if the iron content of a mother's breast milk is lower than that in formula, a baby who is exclusively breast-fed is seldom at risk for iron-deficiency anemia because the iron in breast milk is absorbed at a higher rate. And babies who are formula-fed are also seldom at risk for iron deficiencies because most formulas are iron-fortified. The best thing you can do is consult with your pediatrician about your baby's need for additional iron. Your pediatrician is likely to test baby's iron levels as part of his or her regular checkups at six and/or nine months.

It *is* true that iron-deficiency anemia is the number one nutritional concern in infants, but the babies most at risk fall into the following categories:

> Introducing solids too early may interfere with iron absorption and may lower a baby's iron levels; most often this is related to breast-fed babies.
>
>

- Babies who were born prematurely (iron stores build in the last few months of pregnancy)
- Babies who had a low birth weight even though they were born "full term"
- Infants whose mothers had iron-deficiency anemia, were of poor nutritional status during pregnancy, or had diabetes

The importance of consulting with your baby's pediatrician about the need for iron-fortified cereal and/or iron supplements cannot be stressed enough. All babies are different, and generalities may not apply to your baby.

The Four-Day-Wait Rule

Whether you choose to make baby food or purchase commercial baby food, it is best to abide by the "four-day-wait" rule: introduce your baby to one food at a time and wait approximately four days to introduce the next food. That way, if your baby has a negative reaction to a food, you'll be able to quickly pick out the offending food and eliminate it from baby's diet. Once you have introduced several new foods without a reaction, you can begin to mix them together.

Allergic reactions typically will occur within the first twenty-four hours after you introduce a new food. Digestive issues with new foods may take longer to appear.

When your baby is around eight to ten months old, you will have introduced many new foods and will have a good idea which foods may be allergenic or cause your little one digestive upsets. At this stage you can be less strict about applying the four-day-wait rule. However, it is still important to pay attention to the new foods you offer your little one, especially those that pose an allergy risk.

A few pediatricians have suggested that there is no need to wait between introducing one food and another and that it is fine to introduce baby to several foods at a time. On balance, though, there is no downside to following the rule, especially during the first few weeks of beginning solids. You should decide whether you want to follow, or not follow, the rule based on your baby's family history of food allergies and your baby's overall digestive behaviors. In particular, babies who have a family history of or a particular risk of food allergies will benefit most from the four-day-wait rule.

Introducing Solid Foods: Food Stages and Developmental Stages

As your baby matures, she will continue to develop and reach many wonderful milestones. Feeding stages are part of this process, of course, and the variety of reactions you will encounter at each stage will often delight you even as they prove challenging. For example, two of the most popular are the "I want to feed myself!" stage and the "refusal to eat" stage. Just remember that you are fostering and building healthy eating habits for your little one. This knowledge should help keep you moving happily forward, even if your baby refuses to eat her favorite food and you are cleaning up the fourth spilled bowl of yogurt and fruit in one day.

Keep in mind that the ages listed for each stage are ranges, and there is a fair amount of overlap for the different phases. It is impossible to pinpoint the specifics for all infants because, as noted, infants begin solid foods at different ages, so their progression through the various solid food stages may differ greatly. Part II of this book provides plenty of easy and delicious recipes for you to try in each of these stages.

Four to Six Months—Let's Start Eating!

You have already read a bit about good first food choices and foods to avoid; now let's talk a little about feeding. When baby is first starting solids, the food you offer should be relatively thin and a bit runny. Start out slowly and prepare one or two tablespoon-sized portions of whatever food you have chosen to start with. To take the edge off baby's hunger, nurse or bottle-feed before offering your little one solids. Milk continues to be more important than any solid foods at this age. Some parents begin offering their babies solid foods by using their (clean and washed) finger as a spoon. They say that this helps their babies enjoy and take to solid foods more easily. They feel that introducing the "new" spoon and the "new" food all at once can confuse or overwhelm their baby.

Baby cereal and soft-cooked, thinly pureed fruits and veggies should be baby's first solid food experiences. Offer your baby single ingredients only, and offer each new food four days apart (remember the four-day-wait rule). You may skip the cereal and begin with a fruit like avocado or with a veggie like butternut squash or sweet potato. Try the avocado recipe on page 107 or sweet potatoes on page 111.

Important Note for Parents of Premature Babies

If your baby was born prematurely, it is a good idea to double-check with your pediatrician about the best age to introduce solid foods.

When determining the appropriate age and stage that a "preemie" should begin eating solid foods, using a baby's "corrected age" or "adjusted age" is commonly recommended. The corrected age is determined by taking baby's current age and subtracting the number of weeks/months that the baby was born early. For example, a six-month-old baby who was born eight weeks premature will have a corrected age of around four months.

Six to Eight Months—We're Moving On!

If your six-to-eight-month-old baby is just starting solids, the food you offer should still be relatively thin and a bit runny. Again, start slowly and prepare one or two tablespoon-sized portions of whatever food you have chosen to start with. Your baby might be crawling and trying to pull herself up as she nears eight months old. If she has been eating like a champ and now suddenly refuses to eat, you may wonder if you're raising a picky eater. Don't worry: at this stage baby is simply too busy exploring her world to stop for anything else. In fact, she may get quite miffed when you put her in her high chair to have a meal.

With her independence growing, she may also begin to show preferences for certain foods and may start refusing to be spoon-fed. Why not give her the spoon and let her start to practice? Take heart—this stage of baby feeding, while challenging, will soon pass. Let your baby be your guide and try not to get frustrated. It's important for her to feel that she has some say in which foods she eats, so offer a healthy variety and rest assured she will get everything she needs.

This age/stage also ushers in the dawn of spices (see page 128), textures, and adventure. Start cooking with some spices and slowly add mashed or chopped bits of fruits, vegetables, and meats. Remember, baby will not have molars until sometime around twelve months of age. Foods should be easily squished between the gums. If you haven't done so yet, try offering raw fruits (pureed or mashed and carefully peeled, pitted, and seeded as needed) at this stage. (Try Mango Madness, page 137.) While you may have already introduced yogurt, cheese makes a great addition to baby's diet. See, for example, my recipe for Cottage Peaches on page 165. This is also a great time to try pasta and myriad grains such as quinoa and kamut that are super-tasty and nutritious. Pasta, veggies, and fruit should all be soft-cooked and possibly mashed with a fork or masher. Meats and proteins such as egg yolk should be cooked and pureed or chopped into small, soft bits. If offering tofu, you need not cook it first.

Eight Months and Up—We're Almost Toddlers Now and We Want Grown-up Foods!

By this age/stage, your baby is on the brink of, or may already be, eating "table foods." He may love self-feeding and enjoy a variety of tasty spices and textures in his cuisine. Check out the popular Apple Turkey Loaf or Sticks recipe on page 275 for a great combination of protein, vegetables, fruits, and spices. Now is a great time to encourage a healthy exploration of new foods, tastes, and textures as well as eating utensils. At this time, your baby has likely found a few favorite foods. He may also have developed a preference for feeding himself and a distaste for thin, runny purees. Like the six-to-eight-month-old baby, he may suddenly refuse to eat, but it is rarely a cause for concern. He's simply too busy playing and exploring to stop and eat. Trust your baby's hunger instincts and watch his cues; babies will never starve themselves, so don't worry too much about this refusal to eat.

With his independence growing, baby may begin to show a strong preference for certain foods and may even start refusing anything but his favorite foods. Continue to expand his palate by offering new foods and flavors, and don't get stressed about how much is being eaten. Experiment with new spices and new flavorful combinations, like the Dirty Rice recipe on page 243 and others in stage three. Offer your budding foodie a yummy chicken curry or tasty fish, for example! (An all-time favorite, Simple, Fantastic Fish, is on page 222.)

In the appendix of this book, you will find charts of the foods that are appropriate for the different stages and ages. And the recipes in part II have been presented in three sections corresponding to each of the stages (with their appropriate age ranges).

Now that you have read all about introducing solids, the various first food choices, and the stages of progression, it's time to actually feed your baby. Just remember: Take it slow, keep it simple, and have fun! Your baby will make all kinds of faces that you may not have seen before, and you will probably go through the motions of scraping the food off her chin and back into her mouth quite a few times (not to mention off the high chair, the floor, your clothes...). Keep your cool and your sense of humor—it can come in very handy. Many parents like to capture these moments in photos, so have your camera ready as well. Lights, camera, action!

CHAPTER TWO

Feeding Your Baby Solid Foods—
Let the Fun Begin!

❧✿❧ Grab the dog, a plastic suit, a dropcloth, a mop, and plenty of napkins: here is where the fun and the folly of feeding your baby begins! Actually, you probably won't need the aforementioned accessories until a few weeks after baby has been eating solid foods. In the very beginning stage of introducing solid foods, he will not be eating a lot of food, nor will he be making a huge mess, as you will be in control of the spoon. Things change when your little one moves on to "table foods" and begins to show interest in feeding himself. At that point, you can say good-bye to calm and controlled mealtimes and bid a fond farewell to neatness and clean floors, too. When your baby is self-feeding, all bets are off and you'll be running to find solace and friendship in those cloths and the mop. These will become steadfast allies, as it is likely that more food will be in baby's hair, on his clothes, on the chair, and on the floor than will be in his tummy!

Now that you're ready for that exciting first feeding, it's time to decide what solid food you are going to start with and when you are going to start. In chapter one, several different options for baby's first food were outlined. Beginning with a vegetable like sweet potato is a great choice because it is easily digested and most babies find the taste pleasant; if your baby doesn't like it at first, you can eat it for dinner. Of course, the choice of food is yours to make, and you should talk it over with your baby's pediatrician as well.

There are a few important things you should know before you begin this adventure into solid foods. For instance, watch out for adverse reactions like food allergies, constipation, diarrhea, and other tummy troubles. Learning ahead of time about these curveballs will help keep you from worrying unnecessarily about some issues that may take place.

Rashes and Splotches and Hives, Oh My!

When your baby starts to eat solid foods, you may encounter new rashes, fussiness or splotches, and even the occasional odd-looking poop. Your first thought will probably be, "Oh no, my baby is allergic to [xyz food]?" Don't let yourself become overly concerned that your little one is doomed to live a life hampered by food allergies just yet. Unfortunately, food allergies and preventing them are two of the biggest concerns that parents have when it's time for their babies to start eating solid foods. It is likely that any reactions will not be related to true food allergies. The truth is that just 2 to 6 percent of all children in the United States actually have true food allergies, and many of these allergies may be outgrown. You may have heard that delaying the introduction of certain allergenic foods like

A reaction to a new food might just be a temporary intolerance and not necessarily an allergy to the food.

eggs and wheat will help prevent food allergies. While this used to be the standard recommendation, recent studies have shown that delaying the introduction of many allergenic foods might *not* make a difference in the later development of atopic diseases (like eczema, hay fever, and asthma), although it is important to note that these studies do not take into consideration anaphylactic reactions. What this means is that waiting to offer your baby eggs until she is twelve months old might not prevent an allergy to eggs. Prior to the release of these studies in 2008, most pediatricians advised parents to wait to feed their baby any potentially allergenic foods until after he turned twelve months old. At the time of publication of this book, the American Academy of Pediatrics and pediatricians are rethinking the "old school" recommendations when it comes to allergenic foods. The "new school" of thought is that it might be more beneficial to offer your baby a greater variety of foods earlier, including nutrient-rich allergenic foods such as eggs, than it is to exclude these foods for a twelve-month period of time.

Following are the top eight foods that most commonly cause allergic reactions of one sort or another, for babies and adults alike:

- Cow's milk
- Eggs
- Fish
- Peanuts
- Shellfish

- Soy
- Tree nuts (walnut, cashew, etc.)
- Wheat

But there's good news: Many children outgrow allergies to eggs and milk and even to other foods. On the following table, you will see a list of what I like to call "forbidden foods." These are foods that you might want to wait to introduce to your baby either because they are allergenic or because they may pose other health risks such as botulism or rashes due to high acidity. The table also outlines the age recommendations for introducing these foods to your baby. The "forbidden foods" table notes where current recommendations have changed according to new AAP research and guidelines and also keeps the older recommendations should you decide to take a more conservative approach to introducing the foods listed.

Forbidden Foods

The following chart takes into consideration the new studies and changing recommendations from the American Academy of Pediatrics. Please be sure to ask your pediatrician about introducing "forbidden foods" to your baby.

Food Type and Age for Introduction	Old Recommendation	Current Recommendation
Honey Not an allergen but may cause botulism in infants under 1 year old	After 1 year	After 1 year
Peanuts/ Peanut Butter	After 1 or 2 years	Between 6 months and 2 years

continued

Food Type and Age for Introduction	Old Recommendation	Current Recommendation
(Tree) Nuts Besides being a possible allergen, also may pose a choking hazard	After 1 or 2 years	Between 6 months and 2 years
Citrus or Acidic Fruits Not an allergen but may cause rash and digestive upset due to acidity	After 1 year	Between 6 months and 12 months
Berries Raw strawberries, raspberries, blueberries, and cranberries not included	After 1 year	Between 6 months and 12 months
Corn Possible allergen and not very nutrient-rich	After 10 months to 1 year	Between 6 months and 12 months
Egg Whites	After 1 year	Between 6 months and 12 months
Whole Milk (as a drink) Milk of any type, such as 1% or 2%, should not replace breast milk and/or formula until after 1 year.	After 1 year	After 12 months— whole milk only
Wheat	After 9–10 months or 1 year	Between 6 months and 12 months

Food Type and Age for Introduction	Old Recommendation	Current Recommendation
Grapes Not a high allergen but may pose a choking hazard— use extreme caution if offering your older infant or toddler grapes as snacks.	After 10 months or 1 year	After 10 months or 12 months
Shellfish/Crustaceans May be a potentially deadly allergen; please consult your baby's pediatrician	After 1 or 2 years	Between 6 months and 12 months

Spotting an Allergic Reaction

There are several signs and symptoms to watch out for that may indicate your baby has a potential allergy or intolerance to a food. Many may also occur because of environmental factors such as laundry soap, illness, or even teething. The odd appearance of a rash might be due simply to the acidity of foods like kiwi, oranges, or even tomatoes; sensitivity to the acidity of fruits is common in babies younger than ten to twelve months of age. Gassiness is another symptom that is often due to temporary food intolerance and not to an actual food allergy. Your baby may become gassy because his immature digestive system is reacting to and trying to process a newly introduced food. Digestive upsets tend to be nothing more than temporary tummy troubles rather than an actual food allergy or food intolerance; think of the way broccoli makes many adults gassy. Here are the signs that your baby may have an allergy to a food:

- Sudden loose stools or diarrhea
- Vomiting
- Sudden rashes or red splotches on the skin and bottom
- Runny nose
- Hives
- Irritability and/or gassiness after a new food or meal
- Breathing or other respiratory troubles after a new food/meal
- Swelling of the face, lips, and/or tongue
- Closure or tightening of the throat

Of all the above signs, the closure or tightening of the throat is the most difficult to determine in babies. If your baby's face begins to swell, then it is *possible* that his throat is beginning to tighten and close also; seek immediate attention if swelling occurs. Watch for these symptoms, note the food that you have fed your little one, and continue to keep a close watch on your baby to see if the symptoms progress or subside. Breathing or other respiratory difficulties as well as swelling should be reported immediately.

Always contact your baby's pediatrician if you are feeling unsettled about a possible reaction, and be sure to discuss any symptoms that do not clear up within a twenty-four-hour period.

The Scoop on Poop

It's a delicate topic and one that we're often reluctant to discuss. But when a new baby is welcomed into the family, we suddenly lose all inhibition when it comes to discussing poop. Much to our surprise, we find ourselves in deep conversations with complete strangers about the current color and texture of our baby's poop. It is an important topic for all new parents because you can learn a lot about your baby's digestive health just from looking at and smelling her poop. Up until the time your baby starts eating solid foods, her poops will be fairly regular (even if she poops only a few times a week) and uniform in appearance, texture, and smell. Breast-fed babies often have poop that is naturally a bit runny or grainy, with a smell that some say is sweet. You may have heard that the breast-fed baby has poop that resembles a runny egg or looks like runny cottage cheese and is often a slight greenish or pale yellow color. Formula-fed babies typically have stronger-smelling, thicker poop that may be gray to tan in color. Whether you are breast-feeding or formula-feeding, your baby's poop will go through some dramatic changes once solid foods are introduced. Breast-fed babies seem to have the biggest changes, with smell being the most notable, while formula-fed babies may have more subtle changes.

The Color of Poop

Baby's poop not only changes in composition and fragrance, it often changes in color as well. The vast majority of these color changes are benign and due to the new solid foods that baby is being fed. Here's a small rundown of the possible changes in color and the foods that may contribute to them:

Gray Poop: Blueberries—poop may turn a grayish color and may have small "flecks." These flecks are most likely from blueberry skins.

"Worms" in Tan Poop: Bananas—poop may turn a dark tannish color and also have flecks in it. Some parents describe these flecks as "worms." These little scary-looking things in baby's poop are really harmless. Have a good look at a banana

the next time you peel and mash it; do you see the little flecks of black/brown? Those are the long fibrous seed strings of the bananas.

Orange Bits or "Swirls": Carrots—may not effect a total color change; they may pass just as they went in! This can happen if you have made carrots a bit more chunky and/or thick, but there is no cause for alarm. The next time you make carrots for your baby, try mashing or pureeing them to a smoother texture.

Green Poop: Veggies—sometimes babies can have greenish poop that is a result of eating green veggies. Iron supplements may also cause poop to turn a bit dark green. If food is passing through the intestines too quickly, green poop can result. Bile is what causes poop to be brown, but if the food is going straight through, then bile never gets a chance to work its color magic. This is usually benign, but if it's a common occurrence, you should consult your pediatrician. Greenish poop could also be a sign of trouble; dairy intolerance, an intestinal virus, or Crohn's disease could be the cause.

Red/Pink Poop: Beets—it is possible that some red foods could cause baby's poop to turn a rosy reddish color. However, if you see streaks of red, this could be blood and you should call your doctor immediately! (See below for more information regarding red streaks.)

Some color changes in poop are not benign, and you should contact baby's pediatrician right away if you see them:

White Poop: White poop is not caused from foods, so contact your pediatrician if your baby begins to have white poop.

Black Poop: I have never heard of nor do I know of any foods that turn poop black. Iron, however, may turn poop a dark green, almost black color. Black poop that is tarry may be a sign of intestinal issues, so it is important to have a poop talk with your pediatrician.

Red Blood–Streaked Poop: If baby has reddish or rust-colored streaks in his poops, this could be a sign of a possible medical problem with either the bowels or the intestines. Blood on, but not throughout, poop could be caused from a tear in the anus. A tear may occur if your baby has had a particularly hard or large bowel movement. If you ever see streaks of red, there might be blood in baby's poop and you should call your doctor immediately! Streaks of red blood will be unmistakable: you will see lines of red blood in the poop.

Gassiness, Constipation, and Diarrhea

Introducing solid foods can sometimes upset baby's tummy a bit even if you are introducing foods slowly and waiting until baby is six months of age. Your little one may experience gassiness and/or constipation and diarrhea when he begins to eat solid foods. Constipation and diarrhea are two of the more common upsets that may occur as your baby's digestive system learns to process solid food. While many pediatricians are now suggesting that any and all foods are appropriate to offer baby when starting

> Remember the BRAT diet—bananas, rice, applesauce, and toast. BRAT is used to relieve diarrhea, so cutting out these foods will help relieve constipation.

on solids, you may want to wait a bit to introduce foods that are known to cause digestive upsets. Broccoli, for example, might not be a great first food; it is known to cause gassiness in many adults. Waiting to offer this vegetable until baby is around eight months old might be beneficial, as her intestines will be more mature and might be better able to digest broccoli. Rice and bananas are great starter foods for baby, but too many servings of them may cause your little one to become constipated. Likewise, serving your baby an abundance of foods that are known to loosen stools (peaches, plums, apricots, pears, and fruit juices) might provoke an uncomfortable episode of diarrhea.

Diarrhea

Diarrhea has many causes, the most common being bacteria, viruses, parasites, medications, functional bowel disorders, and food sensitivities. As diarrhea may be a sign of food sensitivity, pay close attention to what baby is eating as you are introducing solid foods. You may have heard of the BRAT diet (bananas, rice, applesauce, and toast), which is used to help alleviate diarrhea. Try rice cereal, applesauce, bananas, and even potatoes if diarrhea occurs. Some doctors say the BRAT diet isn't needed, but they will generally recommend smaller meals whether you use it or not. This will allow his digestive system to work slowly: his tiny intestines and fragile digestive system will take a bit of time (three to four days) to get back on track and healed properly. Always notify and consult with your pediatrician when your baby has diarrhea. Babies who have prolonged bouts of diarrhea will dehydrate easily, and diarrhea in conjunction with a fever lasting longer than seventy-two hours could be a symptom of an illness that needs medical treatment.

Constipation

True constipation is often more difficult to detect than diarrhea. Infrequent pooping is not necessarily a symptom of constipation, as for some babies pooping only twice a week can be normal. Babies who are truly constipated will poop very infrequently and off of their "regular" schedule. Their stools will be very hard and might also have a tarlike texture. If a baby is truly constipated, then she will have a lot of discomfort and difficulty when she is struggling to pass these stools. She may grunt, groan, and even show signs of pain. Just remember that infrequent poops are not necessarily a sign of constipation, but very hard and painful stools most likely indicate that your baby is indeed constipated. Here are a few simple remedies that you might try to get things moving again. Believe it or not, simple exercises may help to relieve baby's current bout of constipation. These exercises are appropriate for babies of all ages:

Tummy Massage: Gently massage and rub baby's tummy in a clockwise direction. Place your hands at baby's navel and massage in a circular motion, moving your hand(s) out and away from the center of baby's belly.

Warm Bath: Some medical professionals suggest that giving your constipated baby a warm bath might be extremely helpful. The thought is that this may help relax baby and her bowels. Why not also give her a tummy massage as you are drying her?

Bicycle Legs: Place your baby on her back and lightly hold her legs in a half-bent position. Begin gently to move your baby's legs as if she is riding a bicycle. Alternate the bicycle legs with tummy massage. Bicycle legs also may help to relieve a baby who is gassy.

Relieving Constipation in Babies Younger Than Four Months

You can try giving your baby one to two ounces of diluted fruit juice daily until her bowels get back to normal. Fruit juices such as pear, apple, or prune offered twice daily should have baby's bowels back to regular in a day or two. When using juice to help alleviate constipation, be sure not to overdo; you want to ensure that baby still has plenty of room to fill her tummy with breast milk and/or formula. You should also continue to practice some of the exercises previously mentioned, as the combination of juice and exercise tends to work well. And always consult your pediatrician about the appropriateness of any new foods and juices that you may use to help ease your baby's constipation.

Relieving Constipation in Babies Four to Twelve Months

Offering your baby strained foods that are high in fiber will help put her bowels back on track. Feeding fruits and veggies such as apricots, prunes, peaches, plums, pears, peas, and even spinach will add some fiber to baby's diet, which is important to help maintain bowel regularity. Barley or oatmeal cereals and most vegetables are preferred foods when a baby is constipated. Juices can also be particularly helpful in easing constipation in older babies, but please be sure to use them in moderation. Juice is not as nutritious for babies as formula or breast milk, and you don't want to fill baby's tummy with so much juice that he won't have room to meet his daily milk requirements. If your baby has just begun to eat solids, you may want to avoid foods such as rice cereal, applesauce, and bananas, as these are known to cause and/or further aggravate constipation.

Baby's First Solid Food Meal—When is a good time to start?

Once you have decided which food you are going to start with, the next step is to decide when to actually take the plunge. Pick a quiet time and place to feed your little one. Think about making baby's first introduction to solid food during the mid-morning or early afternoon. Many parents choose to feed their little ones at dinnertime or even right before they go to sleep for the night, but choosing the evening to feed baby her first few meals might not be the best time. Adults have difficulty digesting a late meal, and babies might have even more difficulty. Remember, baby's tummy is not used to digesting solids, and bellyaches might make her uncomfortable and/or keep her up all night long. As your grandmother told you, "Never go to bed on a full stomach." Your little one may also be tired from a full day and not appreciate being put into a high chair to have a new and foreign substance put into her mouth.

There's one more benefit to introducing new foods during the midmorning or early afternoon. Should there be an adverse reaction, it will cause the least amount of disruption in your baby's fragile routine. You will be able to watch what's going on and deal with any adverse reaction(s) when your pediatrician's office is open. If, for example, your baby suddenly develops a strange rash or begins to vomit a short time after eating a new food, you will monitor the situation at home. If need be, you should be able to get an immediate appointment at your doctor's office, and skipping a trip to the emergency room in the evening would be a big relief!

Preparing Food for Baby's First Feeding

Here are a few points about preparing the food you will be giving your budding foodie:

- If you have made boxed cereal your first food choice, mix a small serving according to the directions on the package and warm as needed.
- If you have chosen to start with jarred food, spoon out a small portion into a separate bowl and heat as desired. Don't feed your baby directly from the jar, as saliva will contaminate the food and you will have to throw away any leftovers.
- For those who are feeding baby homemade food and using the "food cube" method (see page 70), place one cube into a small bowl and thaw or heat as needed.
- If you have chosen to begin with banana or avocado, simply peel and pit as needed, then grab a bowl, place the food into the bowl, and mash it with a fork. Banana and avocado do not need to be cooked, nor do they need to be heated.

Whether you are using homemade or jarred baby foods, you'll want to make sure that the texture and temperature will be pleasing to your baby. The texture should be thin and a bit runny. A good food temperature is one that is either lukewarm or just at room temperature. Another important item to note when introducing solid foods is to give your baby the breast or bottle before the solids. At this stage, formula and/or breast milk will be more important than solids foods, and taking the edge off baby's hunger may just allow him to be more accepting of the new food.

Remember, these first feedings will be entirely new experiences for a baby who is accustomed to drinking liquids only.

When you do start to feed your baby solid foods, never leave him unattended when he is eating (you knew this already, but I wanted to remind you anyway). Why not feed baby with the whole family instead of all by himself in his high chair? Place the high chair or feeding seat at the family table and allow him to sit with everyone even if he is not going to be eating. This will help him become accustomed to mealtime routines. Your baby will enjoy being part of the action at the table.

Use a Comfy Utensil or Your Finger When Feeding Your Baby

Always use a soft and comfy spoon. Remember that baby's gums may be tender from teething, and a hard metal spoon may aggravate them. If he refuses the spoon or if the spoon seems to make him uncomfortable, use your finger. Many parents begin offering their babies solid foods by using their (clean and washed) finger as a spoon.

Don't make a fuss over the food. Talk about the food you are offering and make some "yum yum" sounds, but don't overwhelm your baby with this chatter. This may detract his attention from the food and overstimulate him. Follow your baby's cues and allow him to explore the dish, the utensils, and the food itself. I always gave my babies their own spoon and a little bowl of food as I fed them. And yes, there was lots of food in places other than the babies' mouths! This is one of the downsides to allowing baby a positive exploration of foods, but it is also one of the most important things you can do to help encourage a healthy love of food.

Look at that Little Face—what have I done?

I have to admit that one of my favorite experiences about introducing solids to my babies was watching their little faces as they tasted each bite of a new food. They would come up with so many different expressions that I assigned each face a name. There was the "Are you trying to poison me?" face, which is one you will likely encounter during those first feedings. You'll know this expression immediately: baby's eyes will close, her nose will scrunch up, and her lips will purse tightly together. This facial expression may be accompanied by a lopsided frown and some tiny tears as well. Take heart, this does not mean that your baby doesn't like the food. She likely is just not impressed with the experience of being fed this new substance. With luck, you'll see plenty of the "Oh, this is yummy!" face: baby's eyes will light up and you'll see the thought wheel turning as the food is swished around in her mouth. She may even make soft "mmm" sounds and lean in eagerly toward the spoon.

Studies show it may take a baby between ten and fifteen times of trying a food before a true like/dislike is established. Keep in mind that food likes and dislikes will change constantly as your baby grows.

Now that we're eating, when do we stop?

One typical challenge when feeding a baby solid food is determining when he is full and thus when to stop offering him more. When you are bottle-feeding your baby, you have a good sense of exactly how much he is drinking, as bottles are clearly marked and measured in ounces. You can feel confident knowing that the amount he is drinking will adequately nurture his growing body. Nursing moms are also keenly aware of how much their babies are eating and will know when they are finished with a meal. Feeding your baby solids and determining when he is full is a bit like driving to a new location without the benefit of a map or a GPS. At this point, you may find yourself wondering once again why babies don't come with instructions and why your doctor or hospital didn't give you maps and a compass when you left with your precious bundle of joy! The truth is, you really don't need to fret, nor do you need precise instructions. You'll hear it often and from many people, including the pediatrician: Trust your baby to let you know when he is full. The vast majority of pediatricians will all say, "Feed your baby as much as your baby will eat." One of the cave-ats to this is that when you are feeding your baby solid foods, you should ensure that he is still receiving the proper amounts of breast milk and/or formula.

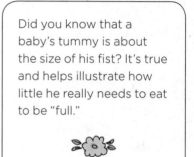

Did you know that a baby's tummy is about the size of his fist? It's true and helps illustrate how little he really needs to eat to be "full."

Here are some signs that baby may want to continue to eat:

- Leaning in for the spoon.
- Opening the mouth for more.
- Grabbing for food and trying to put it in the mouth.

Some signs that your baby may be full:

- The "mouth clamp" baby closes her mouth as the spoon comes close. But be careful, this sign is also one you will see when baby truly dislikes a certain taste!
- Spitting out food.
- Turning the head away as the spoon comes closer.

Solid foods in the early stage are meant for practice. Unlike breast milk and/or formula, solid foods are not meant to provide your baby's total nutrition. Don't stress about a lack of interest in solid foods!

As all pediatricians will tell you, your baby will never starve herself. The majority of healthy babies will eat just the right amount of foods that they need. Offering a well-balanced diet of solid foods will help ensure that your baby is eating the right amount of the right nutritious foods.

Resist the urge to offer "just one more bite" when your baby indicates she's finished. You do not want to accidentally override your baby's developing ability to self-regulate her feeding by continuing to feed her. It is important to pay close attention to your baby's cues, as her feeding patterns will change daily and may be affected by the goings-on around her. A healthy and well-fed baby should be producing wet diapers regularly and one or two bowel movements during the day.

Don't forget that your baby is just a little human being, and like all of us, she has her own appetite. This will always influence how much solid food she will be eating. Like adults, some babies will eat more than others owing to their individual appetites. Following are a few key points to remember when feeding your baby.

- A six-month-old baby who began solid foods at four months of age will most likely be eating more solid foods than a six-month-old baby who is just beginning to eat solids.
- A baby who is skipping the purees and eating soft diced foods may seem to eat less than the baby who is being spoon-fed purees.
- A baby who is ill or teething may for a few days eat less than what has been typical, and then suddenly the typical appetite will come roaring back.
- An infant who is busy exploring the carpet or the new book she has received may be miffed when she is put into a high chair and offered food.
- The natural slowdown of growth that babies go through will influence how much they eat. They may be ravenous for a few days or a week or two, and then suddenly they are barely eating.

Sample Schedule for Introducing Solid Foods

Keep in mind that you will probably manage to feed your baby only half of a tablespoon-sized portion the first times you begin solids. Once you have introduced a variety of foods, you can make baby meals and combinations with the foods that she has been eating. Please note that the combinations offered here are intended to give you an idea of how to introduce several foods over a few weeks. You may substitute any of the first foods outlined on page 99 for what is written here.

Week 1: avocado and/or sweet potato. Offer these foods for three or four days and then move to another food. Try one tablespoon for the first few feedings and let your baby be your guide.

Week 2: banana and/or pears (include avocado and/or sweet potato). Continue feeding small amounts, as baby will still be getting used to solid foods. Offer these foods for three or four days, then move to another food.

Week 3: butternut squash and/or apples (include banana and/or pears, avocado, and sweet potato). Continue feeding your baby small amounts. By now, you should know how solid foods are affecting baby's digestion, and her bowel movements may have begun to change. Offer these foods for three or four days, then move to another food.

Week 4: green beans and/or rice cereal (include butternut squash and/or apples, banana, pears, avocado, and sweet potato). Your budding foodie will likely be on a wider variety of foods now. Expand her palate by becoming more creative with mixing foods. Offer these foods for three or four days, then move to another food.

Week 5: peaches and/or plums (include green beans, rice cereal, butternut squash, avocado, bananas, pears, sweet potatoes, and apples). Offer these foods for three or four days, then move to another food; just look at all the foods your baby has now been eating!

CHAPTER THREE

Nutritional Information

We need many different nutrients to help our bodies grow strong and function properly. For babies, a number of these are crucial to ensuring proper development and growth. While many parents might obsess over the proper amount of nutrients, rest assured that your baby will likely be receiving all that he or she needs without any nutritional intervention at all. If you are breast-feeding and/or formula-feeding, these two sources provide all the fats, vitamins, minerals, and other nutrients that a baby needs. Adding a well-rounded and balanced diet of solid foods serves only to complement and enhance the nutrition received from milk. It is most important to offer your baby a well-rounded diet of foods so that you decrease the likelihood of needing to use supplements. This chapter will discuss the importance of different vitamins, minerals, fats, and proteins for babies at different stages of growth. You'll also find a useful breakdown of nutrients and the best food sources for getting those nutrients into your baby's diet.

Minerals (Iron, Zinc, Calcium)

Minerals are an important part of a healthy diet, just as vitamins and other nutrients are. Minerals are found throughout the natural world, not only in the foods we eat but also in the makeup of planet Earth itself; sand, stone, plants, and water. For the human body, minerals are key building blocks of healthy cells and tissue such as muscles, cartilage, and even the human brain. The following pages will explore various minerals that are very important for growing babies.

Iron

Iron plays a critical role in helping to maintain healthy red blood cells and carry oxygen through our blood. It also helps the body's immune system function properly by defending us against bacteria, viruses, and other unsavory pathogens that could make us ill. It is not commonly known that iron also plays a role in metabolism, regulating the body's temperature, and it even helps to ensure healthy cognitive development. Iron is one of the most important nutrients that a developing baby needs. As mentioned in chapter one, the vast majority of babies will not become iron-deficient if they do not eat a fortified baby rice cereal, nor will they become iron-deficient if they do not receive supplements unless there are underlying factors such as pre-

> To help with the absorption of iron, serve foods containing vitamin C with a meal. For example, make Creamy Peachy Chicken and Rice (page 179), a meal that is packed full of iron and vitamin C.

term birth, low birth weight, or a mother who suffered from nutritional deficiencies during pregnancy.

Iron is found in two different forms, heme and non-heme. Heme iron is the form that our bodies best absorb and use most efficiently. It makes up about 40 percent of the iron in meat, poultry (including eggs, in particular the yolks), and fish. Non-heme iron is present in animal tissue and makes up all of the iron in plants (fruits, vegetables, grains, nuts). Non-heme iron is not absorbed or utilized by the body as well as heme iron.

How much iron does a baby need, and what foods should I offer?

According to the National Institutes of Health (United States), the recommended daily allowance (RDA) for infants from birth to six months of age is 0.27 milligrams (mg) of iron per day. For babies seven to twelve months, the RDA for iron increases to 11 mg per day. When a baby reaches the age of one year, the RDA actually decreases to 7 mg per day. Once children reach the age of four to eight years, the RDA for iron goes back up to 10 mg per day. These daily recommendations apply to both male and female children. Once girls reach the age of fourteen, their iron requirements increase more than those of boys, with the increase continuing to be gender driven up until the age of fifty years. Below is a list of foods that are rich in iron. You should try to serve your infant at least two of these foods every day (ensure that the foods are age-appropriate) once he has begun to decrease his breast milk/formula intake and eat more solid foods.

- breast milk and iron-fortified infant formula
- blackstrap molasses (try adding a little to cereal when baby is over ten months old)

- brewer's yeast
- broccoli
- dried beans
- dried fruit (figs, apricots, prunes, raisins)
- egg yolks
- grains (cooked cracked wheat, wheat germ, cornmeal, millet, brown rice, farina, bran, breads, iron-fortified cereals)
- greens (spinach, broccoli, beets, kale, etc.)
- meat and poultry (beef, beef and chicken liver, pork, turkey, chicken, egg yolks)
- mushrooms
- prune juice
- shellfish (clams, oysters, shrimp)
- sweet potatoes
- tofu
- tuna, sardines, canned salmon
- winter squash

How much iron is in the food I feed my baby?

You may be surprised to see exactly how much iron is in just 1 tablespoon of some common baby foods; 1 tablespoon is equal to approximately 14 grams. Take a look at how much iron is in the following foods, courtesy of the USDA Nutrient Database:*

Broccoli: 0.09 mg
Sweet potato: 0.10 mg
Beef: 0.36 mg

---

*USDA Nutrient Data Laboratory may be accessed at http://www.nal.usda.gov/fnic/foodcomp/search/.

Chicken: 0.15 mg (light meat)
Chicken: 0.19 mg (dark meat)
Egg yolk: 0.38 mg

While the amounts of iron in the previous list may seem small, let's put it into perspective. The RDA for iron for infants between the ages of seven and twelve months is 11 mg. If you are formula-feeding, your baby will receive approximately 1.4 mg with every 2 ounces he drinks. If you are breast-feeding your little one, he may receive less iron; however, the iron he does receive will be more readily available to his body. According to the National Institutes of Health, Office of Dietary Supplements, it is estimated that 50 percent of the iron from breast milk is used and absorbed by babies, while the iron in formula is only 12 percent utilized.* During the day, a nine-month-old may drink 24 to 31 ounces of formula. Assuming he drinks 25 ounces, he would receive approximately 18 mg of iron. So you have met the 11 mg RDA and then some through formula alone. Exceeding the RDA for iron from food or formula/breast milk sources is not harmful; however, overdosing with iron supplements can be dangerous.

In a sample meal of 3 ounces of beef, 2 ounces of sweet potato, and 2 ounces of applesauce, your baby's iron intake would look something like this:

3 oz of beef = 3.2 mg
2 oz of sweet potato = 0.20 mg
2 oz of applesauce = 0.12 mg
Total iron for meal = approximately 3.52 mg

---

* National Institutes of Health, Office of Dietary Supplements, http://ods.od.nih.gov/factsheets/iron/.

Zinc

Zinc, found in the cells of our bodies, plays a large role in the proper growth of our bodies and the normal functioning of our immune systems. Zinc is also important for healing, normal sexual development, and reproduction. Zinc is relatively easy to include in the diet and is found in mushrooms, wheat germ, brewer's yeast, soybeans, pumpkin seeds, sunflower seeds, meats, dairy, oysters, seafood (including crustaceans), legumes, and even eggs. Many pediatricians are recommending that babies be offered meats as a first food (though not necessarily *the* first food) to help stave off a possible (though unlikely) zinc deficiency. You may be surprised to learn that the RDA for zinc is only 3 mg for infants six to twelve months old and that a deficiency in zinc is rare.

Calcium

We all know how important calcium is to the good health of our bones and teeth, but did you know that of all the minerals we have, calcium is found at a higher level in our bodies than any other? Calcium is stored in our bones, teeth, and even muscle and other tissue. It is very important to the growth of healthy bones and those teeth that start coming out around the age of six months. Calcium also helps to build permanent teeth. Your baby will get enough calcium from formula and/or breast milk, and it is only when he's being weaned off these liquids that you need to pay closer attention to calcium needs. Throughout infancy, breast milk will always contain the right amounts of calcium that your growing baby needs; even though breast milk contains less calcium than formula, it is better absorbed (like iron), so that baby does not need as much. Calcium is found in so many foods that if a baby does not drink milk after the age of twelve months, that's not necessarily going to cause a deficiency. Check out the labels of any foods you buy and you will be surprised to see how many contain calcium: yogurt, cottage cheese, hard cheeses, and even cream cheese are wonderful sources of calcium and vitamin D and are very nutritious for your little one. Here are some other foods that contain calcium:

broccoli
canned salmon
certain types of legumes such as kidney beans
fortified orange juice
sweet potatoes
tofu
whole-wheat bread

Protein

If you were asked what protein is, what would be your answer? We all know that we need protein in our diets—protein helps our bodies grow strong, keeps our muscles and tissues healthy, is important for maintaining and repairing our cells, and strengthens our immune systems so that we can produce antibodies to take on germs, viruses, bacteria, and other pathogens that can cause illness. There is no part of our body or bodily function that does not benefit from protein. Did you know that there are actually two types of proteins? "Complete" proteins contain all the essential amino acids, and their best sources are meat, eggs, dairy, and nuts and seeds. "Incomplete" proteins are lacking in one or more of the essential amino acids. Plant foods such as legumes, grains, fruits, and vegetables contain incomplete proteins. Without amino acids, protein would break down and our muscles, tissues, and even cells would weaken and degenerate. When we eat or drink protein, we are helping our bodies obtain amino acids. Amino acids are not stored in the body, so it is important to obtain them daily through diet. Formula and breast milk contain adequate amounts of protein for your baby, but when your baby begins to eat solid foods, it is important to offer her foods that contain protein.

Protein RDA for Infants and Children

Infants up to 1 year	11 grams
Children 1–3 years	13 grams
Children 4–8 years	19 grams

The RDA for protein is based on weight after the age of one year and is calculated at 0.55 gram per pound. Meat is one of the best sources of complete protein; that's an important reason parents are urged to introduce meats at the seven-to-nine-

Quinoa: Did you know that quinoa, while thought of as a grain, is really a seed? Did you know that quinoa is a source of complete protein? It contains all the essential amino acids that our bodies need and makes a wonderful addition to your baby's diet. For a supernutritious, protein-packed meal, make the family a quinoa pilaf that baby can enjoy, too! See Quinoa Vegetable Pilaf with Lemon on page 246.

month age range. Of course, introducing meat into your baby's diet prior to twelve months of age is a personal decision. Protein does not have to come from meat, and meat itself is not a necessity in an infant's diet. Your child can receive all the proteins needed by combining other foods that contain complete and incomplete proteins.

A great example of a few protein-packed "meals" would be peanut butter *(consult your pediatrician about the appropriate age for introducing peanut butter)* and bread, black beans and rice with grated cheddar cheese, cottage cheese with avocado and whole-wheat bread, or milk and any grain cereal. However, before you decide to exclude meat from your child's diet, consider the possible ramifications; consult with your pediatrician and/or a registered dietitian prior to embarking on a "meat-free" or other form of vegetarian/vegan diet for your baby as his first birthday approaches.

Vitamins

When I think about vitamins, I'm always reminded of the *I Love Lucy* episode where Lucy is auditioning for a commercial to sell the vitamin supplement "Vitameatavegamin." She has to do so many takes that she winds up a bit tipsy because the supplement contains a lot of alcohol! Of course, because I was so young, I had no idea about the alcohol-silliness connection. When I watch this hilarious episode now, I get the message that supplements are no substitute for the real thing: fresh whole foods. Getting your daily allowance of vitamins is so easy if you just take the time to eat a balanced variety of nutritious whole foods. The same is true for babies: if fed a well-rounded, balanced, and nutritious diet, they will receive all of the important nutrients they need; most healthy babies should not need to take vitamin supplements. Following is a list of some of the vitamins that are important to help keep your baby healthy and strong.

Vitamin A: Vitamin A is found in a large variety of fruits, vegetables, meats, and even dairy. You may serve carrots, winter squash, sweet potatoes, avocados, spinach, yellow/orange fruits and vegetables, dark green leafy vegetables, kiwi, prunes, papaya, liver, eggs, milk and milk products, and even the spice paprika to get vitamin A. Fat-soluble vitamin A plays an essential role in vision, growth, and development; the maintenance of healthy skin, hair, and mucous membranes; immune functions; and even reproductive functions.

Vitamin C: You can find vitamin C in green and red peppers, avocados, banana, cabbage, kiwi, turnip greens, kale, collards, parsley, sprouted alfalfa seeds, broccoli, tomatoes, mangoes, lemons, oranges, black currants, acerola cherries, cantaloupe, strawberries, and other citrus. (If you love loose-leaf tea, vitamin C is even contained in rose hips.) Vitamin C is important for the formation of collagen, a protein that gives structure to bones, cartilage, muscle, and blood vessels. Vitamin C also aids in the absorption of iron, so be sure to add it to baby's diet often. Vitamin C is said to help fight or stave off colds, and it is thought to remove "free radicals" from the body. Free radicals are atoms that cause a negative chain reaction when they meet up with certain molecules and oxygen, damaging our cells and even our DNA. Antioxidants like vitamin C can inhibit this chain reaction and thus contain or remove free radicals.

Vitamin C is water-soluble, which means that it dissolves in water and can be destroyed by heat and even light. Steaming or baking foods that are rich in vitamin C will help preserve the vitamin, and adding the cooking water back into foods will also help recapture any lost nutrients.

Vitamin D: In recent years, adequate vitamin D intake has become a source of concern as more and more infants and young children are found to be deficient. For instance, there has been an increase in rickets, which occurs when the bones become soft or weak from a lack of vitamin D. Vitamin D is very important for strong bones, and it is essential for normal growth and development. In 2008, the American Academy of Pediatrics recommended that all infants and children, including adolescents, maintain a minimum daily intake of 400 IU of vitamin D beginning shortly after birth. Please be sure to ask your pediatrician about the need for Vitamin D supplementation for your baby. Vitamin D is found in salmon, sardines, herring, tuna, organ meats, vitamin D–fortified milk and milk products, egg yolks, and even wheat germ. In addition, vitamin D may be obtained from exposure to the sun. There are those who theorize that the rise in vitamin D deficiency may be due in part to the copious amounts of sunscreen we use to protect our skin from the harmful effects of the sun. Though important to use, sunscreen has the negative effect of blocking the sun's ability to stimulate vitamin D production in our bodies. Researchers and doctors at the Boston University Medical Center (among others) have been recommending

Wheat germ is an excellent way to boost vitamin D, iron, and even folate levels. Sprinkle on cereals, baked squash, and yogurt. You can also add it to meat loaf, cookies, and many other foods!

that "sensible sun exposure (usually 5–10 minutes of exposure of the arms and legs or the hands, arms, and face, 2 or 3 times per week) and increased dietary and supplemental vitamin D intakes are reasonable approaches to guarantee vitamin D sufficiency."* Exposing your little one to sunlight in the early morning or late afternoon hours (when the sun's rays are less intense) is one way of stimulating vitamin D production without increasing the risk of damaging exposure to the sun.

Folate: Folate, one of the water-soluble B vitamins (B$_9$), helps the body make red blood cells and form the genetic material that is in every cell within our bodies; it also helps our bodies with protein metabolism. It is important to replenish folate each day through the diet. Folate is found in chicken liver, beef liver, fortified breakfast cereals, lentils and chickpeas, asparagus, spinach, black beans, kidney beans, lima beans, tomato juice, brussels sprouts, oranges, broccoli, wheat germ, and fortified white bread.

Fats and Carbohydrates

Just the mention of fats and carbohydrates is enough to send many people into the depths of despair—it's that difficult to think about these two nutrients as being a necessity in a healthy diet. For babies, fats and carbohydrates play a very important nutritional role in growth and development. During their first year of life, they grow rapidly, and carbohydrates provide the continual supply of energy their bodies need. Babies actually burn a lot of calories growing!

---

* Michael Holick, "Sunlight and Vitamin D for Bone Health and Prevention of Autoimmune Diseases, Cancers, and Cardiovascular Disease," *American Journal of Clinical Nutrition* 80 (Suppl. 6) (2004): 1678S–88S.

Fat—specifically, EFAs (essential fatty acids) and unsaturated fat—is important for optimal growth and development, so much so that experts advise against restricting fat in infants and toddlers under the age of two years. There are two forms of EFA: alpha-linolenic acid (an omega-3 fatty acid) and linoleic acid (an omega-6 fatty acid). Our bodies do not naturally produce either one, so both EFAs must be obtained from food sources. Babies will receive the proper amounts of fats via breast milk and/or formula, but when it comes time to introduce solid foods, milk intake will decrease and other sources of fats will play a larger role.

Fresh fruits such as strawberries, nuts and seeds like walnuts and flax, vegetables such as butternut squash, broccoli, and kale, and fish like salmon will provide plenty of omega-3 fatty acids. Cooking with vegetable oils and incorporating seeds and oils from seeds into the diet will offer up a healthy dose of omega-6 fatty acids. Flaxseed, flax oil, and wheat germ can be added to many recipes to boost the omega-3s and fat content.

CHAPTER FOUR

Curiosities and Myths in Baby Feeding

Throughout the generations, advice on feeding babies has continually changed. Much of the advice from past generations ranged from the practical to the professional to the just plain odd. Can you imagine stirring milk and sugar into flour as a substitute for breast milk?

Myth: Nitrates in homemade vegetables are dangerous; commercial baby food is free of nitrates.

You may have been advised by your pediatrician not to make your baby certain types of nitrate-rich foods, like carrots, to avoid the possibility of a certain type of anemia or "nitrate poisoning." Nitrate poisoning may lead to methemoglobinemia, also called "blue baby syndrome," in which the ability of a baby's red blood cells to transport oxygen to the tissues of the body is compromised.

The American Academy of Pediatrics advises against preparing homemade foods from vegetables that contain nitrates (such as carrots, spinach, beets, green beans, and squash) until a baby is at least three months old or older. (In their opinion, it is not necessary to introduce solid foods of any kind before baby is four to six months of age.)* Around the age of six months, an infant's tummy should be developed enough to handle normal nitrate exposure from any homemade foods. Nitrate levels, it should be noted, are found in their highest concentration in well water. Infants truly at risk for nitrate poisoning are those who are being fed formula that is prepared with well water. Households that rely on private wells for their water supply should have the water tested at least once a year.

> There is no government regulation, law, or mandate that forces commercial baby food companies to screen for nitrates. Commercial baby food companies may opt voluntarily to screen their foods for nitrates, but they are not required to do so.

Another common myth associated with nitrates is that commercial baby foods do not contain nitrates because they are screened for nitrates. Yes, commercial baby food companies may screen their vegetable products to ensure that high nitrate levels are not present, but this screening does not *remove* nitrates. Nitrates occur naturally in the soil and even in the vegetables themselves and therefore cannot be removed. More-

---

* "Infant Methemoglobinemia: The Role of Dietary Nitrate in Food and Water," *Pediatrics* 116, no. 3 (September 2005): 784–786 (doi:10.1542/peds.2005-1497).

over, certain foods, such as spinach, beets, cabbage, broccoli, and carrots, tend to accumulate higher nitrate levels than is natural because of soil conditions and/or fertilizers.

Even organic commercial carrot baby foods will contain some nitrate. If you choose organic vegetables, nitrate levels may be significantly reduced, but they will never be eliminated. Remember that the nitrates are naturally occurring, and even farming without using nitrogen fertilizers will not completely eliminate nitrate concentration.

Myth: Baby food must be bland.

The origin of this myth is unknown; however, it could stem from the fact that bland (and boring) rice cereal has long been recommended in the United States, and a few other countries, as the first food babies should be eating. While rice cereal is certainly considered an appropriate first food because of its iron fortification and because it's low on the allergen list, it is unfortunately high on the bland list. There are other, more interesting foods that rival it in nutritional composition. Take the avocado, for example: brimming with important nutrients like vitamins A and C and healthy fats, a mashed avocado is anything but bland and boring in taste and texture. Add a sprinkle

Did you know that your baby is already enjoying these herby and spicy tastes if he is breast-feeding? The flavors of the foods, herbs, and spices that Mom eats pass through her breast milk; many babies already know the taste of garlic or cinnamon or tarragon.

of garlic powder into the avocado mash and your baby's taste buds are awake and paying attention.

Many pediatricians recommend adding spices and herbs to baby's diet around the age of eight months, but the recommendations for introducing solid foods to babies have loosened up significantly; adding herbs and spices early is no longer frowned upon. In fact, it should be encouraged so that babies will learn to appreciate the flavors the rest of the family enjoys. An added benefit of introducing your baby to herbs and spices early and often is that she will be embracing foods enhanced with wholesome additions rather than relying upon foods that are salted and sugared up!

Myth: Babies should not eat dairy like yogurt and/or cheese until twelve months or older.

Thanks to incomplete or conflicting advice given by pediatricians and other health care practitioners, parents and caregivers are often confused when it comes to introducing dairy products to a baby. Yogurt is considered safe to introduce anytime between six and eight months of age, as is cheese (although you must pay close attention to the texture of cheese in all forms, as it may pose a choking hazard).

Infants may begin the transition to drinking whole milk sometime between ten and twelve months old; introducing milk as a drink any earlier could have negative health consequences. The medical community is concerned that if whole cow milk is introduced to an infant prior to one year old, parents might decrease or stop formula- and/or breast-feeding and replace these more nutritious foods with milk. This could be dangerous to your baby's health and growth, particularly since whole cow milk does not contain iron and may in fact limit the ability of the body to absorb iron. However, many pediatricians and doctors neglect to specify the difference between drinking milk and eating dairy products. One of the most interesting reasons yogurt and/or cheese may be introduced earlier is that when yogurt and cheese are cultured, the lactose is broken down and the milk proteins limited, which makes yogurt and cheese easier to digest.

Curiosity: Babies do not need teeth to chew textured or chunky foods.

When it comes time for baby to move on to chunkier foods or table foods, many parents are a bit hesitant, in part because their babies might not have any teeth. It's a common misconception that babies should not start to eat finger foods until they get their teeth. This is logical—after all, we use our teeth to chew foods of harder and chunkier textures. We seldom use our front teeth to actually chew the foods we eat; it is the molars, the big teeth in the back of our mouths, that we use to actually chew our foods. Babies won't get their molars until sometime between twelve and nineteen months of age; that's a long time! However, despite the lack of molars, babies have very strong and tough gums that are capable of mashing and grinding soft-cooked foods of almost any texture with relative ease. If you're unsure about how capable baby's gums are, just ask the nursing mom how it feels when baby clamps down. Try this to test if the food is mashable: Place a piece of any food that you want to offer your baby between your thumb and pointer finger and squeeze it gently. If you can mash the food between your thumb and finger, then your baby's gums can certainly mash that same food. Another thing you might want to do is put the food in your mouth, swirl it around, and push it against your cheek with your tongue; if the food is easily mashed, then your baby can handle it.

Myth: Green vegetables before orange, and never offer fruits before vegetables—ever.

Despite all the research and studies that have been done about the order of introducing solid foods to babies, this is the one myth that continues to hang on. Some pediatricians say to introduce the vegetables first so that your baby does not develop a "sweet tooth" for fruits. But for the breast-fed baby, it's too late: breast milk is a sweet food, which means breast-fed babies get to eat the sweetest food there is, straight from the beginning of life! Some pediatricians advise introducing fruits first, as this approach will help baby enjoy her first foods and she will be less likely to reject them. Then there is the order of vegetable color recommendations. Here's the good news: There is no hard scientific evidence to prove any of these myths. You will find many babies who love their green veggies and totally dislike their fruits. Of course, there are also babies who seem to have a "sweet" tooth and simply prefer the yellow/orange vegetables. It is possible that this might be more of a texture issue than a taste issue; green vegetables (peas, for example) tend to be tougher and not as smooth as the yellow/orange veggies (sweet potato). If you are unsure about all of this, then why not try to introduce foods in an alternating order? Try sweet potatoes, then bananas—then avocados and then peaches, for example. Alternating between a fruit and a vegetable, and maybe some homemade cereal along the way, is a great way to get the best of both worlds!

Curiosity: Babies will turn orange if they are fed an abundance of orange foods.

One day while you are gazing lovingly upon the beautiful child you created, you feel that something is amiss. Suddenly it dawns on you: your baby's nose is orange and, as a matter of fact, so are her cheeks—and oh, my goodness, the palms of her hands are orange, too!

There's no need to panic. Your baby may have carotenemia, a condition that causes the skin to take on an orange tinge because of increased blood carotene levels. In the vast majority of cases seen, this orange tinge is associated with the heavy consumption of foods rich in carotene. It is not uncommon for babies who are fed lots of orange fruits and vegetables to have their palms, soles of the feet, and even face take on a "sun-kissed" hue.

Some orange foods such as sweet potatoes, winter squash, pumpkin, and carrots contain high levels of beta-carotene, which is converted to vitamin A. You can tell how much beta-carotene is in a fruit or veggie by looking at the color: The deeper the color of the orange veggie or fruit, the higher the amount of beta-carotene. Dark green vegetables such as kale, spinach, and broccoli are also high in beta-carotene.

Don't be afraid that your baby will have an orange nose and orange cheeks forever. Decreasing the amount of foods containing beta-carotene will help get his skin back to its usual color. Many parents fear that this unusual orange color might be a symptom of jaundice. Sickly babies are most at risk for jaundice; those who are becoming jaundiced will be looking more yellow than orange, and the whites of the baby's eyes will also be tinged with yellow. If you suspect your baby may have jaundice, speak with your pediatrician as soon as possible.

Myth: Adding cereal to baby's bottle will help him sleep through the night.

Perhaps one of the most worrisome myths is that cereal in a bottle will help a baby sleep through the night (or at least sleep for longer stretches at a time). Many parents are understandably tempted to give this a try to gain a desperately needed hour of sleep. My own twins were not good sleepers; they seldom slept longer than three hours and were not on the same sleeping (or eating) schedule for the first seven months. I was completely sleep deprived. Adding cereal to my babies' bottles was not an option as they were breast-fed and did not take bottles. I also knew that this was not a healthy practice. Still, I longed for a way to get my babies to sleep, on the same schedule, and I always asked my pediatrician if he had any tricks. As my pediatrician would often remind me, "No matter how often or how long you nurse those babies at this age, they will sleep on their own terms and there is absolutely nothing you can do about it." He often spoke about adding cereal to the bottle and how it was a myth.

Unless your baby has been diagnosed with reflux and has a medical need for cereal added to a bottle, you should resist this temptation. Feeding babies cereal in their bottles may throw their "I'm full" instinct off-kilter and put them in danger of overeating; more important, babies have been known to aspirate cereal when it is mixed in a bottle with formula or breast milk. Babies younger than four to six months old seldom know how to properly swallow anything other than breast milk or formula. Gulping or "inhaling" a bottle with cereal in it could have deadly consequences.

One reason parents might think that this strategy works is that they usually try it when their baby is between two and three months old (this seems to be the breaking point of many sleep-deprived parents). As it happens, it is at this age that babies may begin to sleep for longer periods on their own, naturally, and this coincidence seems to perpetuate the myth that cereal in a bottle does indeed help an infant sleep through the night.

Curiosity: Six months is a special age for introducing solid foods to babies.

A few "magical" things happen for babies around four to six months of age that make it the ideal time to introduce solid foods.

- Baby's intestines should be fully "closed"—it is said that the lining of an infant's intestines are "open" and porous. Foreign proteins (such as food particles) may be passed through the intestinal wall if it has not matured and is still open.
- Babies are less likely to aspirate foods.
- Baby is better able to recognize that she is full and regulate how much she needs to eat.
- Baby is able to indicate she is full by turning away from food or firmly closing her mouth as the spoon approaches.
- Baby should have fully developed head control and be able to sit up with minimal assistance.
- Baby has had breast milk or formula during the crucial first six months of life, giving her the healthiest start with optimal nutrients.

Curiosity: Recipes for baby food from the 1800s.

It is always interesting to see how feeding practices have changed over the generations. Some old ones have, thankfully, been abandoned while others have been tweaked and made more healthful thanks to the evolution of the nutritional sciences. Following are two recipes* that illustrate how far science and knowledge have progressed when it comes to feeding babies. The author was quite a "celebrity chef" back in her day. Here is her recipe entitled *Food for a Young Infant*:

> Take of fresh cow's milk one table-spoons full, and mix with 2 table-spoonsfull of hot water; sweeten with loaf-sugar as much as may be agreeable. This quantity if [sic] sufficient for once feeding a new-born infant; and the same quantity may be given every 2 or 3 hours— not oftener—till the mother's breast affords the natural nourishment.

And another, entitled *Thickened Milk for Young Infants When 6 Months Old*:

> Take 1 pint of milk, 1 pint of water; boil it and add 1 tablespoon of flour. Dissolve the flour first in half a tea-cup of water; it must be strained in gradually and boiled hard for 20 minutes. As the child grows older, one-third water. If properly made, it is the most nutritious, at the

---

*These recipes for baby food come from a cookbook published in 1852. The book is called *Cookery for Children* and was written by Sarah Josepha Hale.

same time the most delicate food that can be given to young infants.

This book also recommends stale bread as a staple in the diet as well as liberal amounts of sugar in fruits and vegetables. I wonder what the author would think of her feeding advice and recipes in this day and age, considering the studies and research in nutrition!

CHAPTER FIVE

Making Fresh Homemade Baby Food—Break Out the Food Processor and Turn On the Oven!

So, you're thinking about making homemade baby food. Before you get started, it's important to realize that making homemade baby food is not an "all or nothing" proposition. In today's busy world, it can be next to impossible to find the time to simply sit and rest. If you start to make your baby's food and soon feel overwhelmed or believe that it's just not working out for you, then take a break and regroup. Your baby's taste buds and tummy will surely thank you for all the fresh and wholesome foods that you prepare for him, but he needs a parent who is relaxed and joyful far more than he needs homemade baby

Making homemade baby food is as simple as cooking, pureeing, and storing!

food. This chapter will show you the easiest and most convenient ways to make your baby's food fresh in as little time as possible without feeling like a short-order cook.

Having made food for both twins and a singleton, I learned how essential it was to develop a simple, streamlined, and time-/cost-effective process. With just small additions to your current routine and a few easy steps, it can take as little as one hour per week. Really, I'm not exaggerating! If you have just one hour per week, you can make a large supply of homemade baby food. And you can do it while you're cooking your family meals. Remember, baby food is nothing more than food for grown-ups that has been mashed, blended, or pureed.

A few reasons why making homemade baby food is a wonderful choice

Quality Control: Whether you choose to make organic or conventional foods, when your baby's food is fresh and homemade, you have total control over the ingredients. If your baby is prone to food allergies, you can ensure that no allergenic foods are slipping into baby's meals. You literally handpick and choose!

You Have the Gadgets: Everything you may need to make fresh and wholesome baby food is probably already in your kitchen. Now, this doesn't mean that you can't buy a new gadget or appliance; in fact, making baby's food from scratch might be the excuse you've been looking for to go out and buy that new food processor!

Fresh Foods with Expanded Tastes and Tailored Textures: With homemade food, your baby will be exposed to a greater variety of tastes and textures. Let's be honest, those jarred foods won't come in flavors such as Banana 'Cado (page 108) or Pink Potatoes (page 272)! The texture of homemade baby food might make the transition to table foods a bit less stressful for your baby as well.

Your Baby's Needs on Your Baby's Schedule: In making home-made baby foods, you are the chef who knows exactly what your baby wants and needs. Because you will be controlling the texture and ingredients of her foods, you will know what foods are best suited for your baby at any given stage.

Laying the Foundation for Healthy Eating Habits: Raising babies to prefer the taste of fresh, real, whole foods over highly processed, chemically laden versions is one small step in com-bating childhood obesity. Healthy eating habits will develop far earlier when you expose your baby to a variety of tastes. You will find that you become dedicated to making and feed-ing your little one only high-quality, fresh, wholesome, and nutritious baby foods and snacks. Your baby will benefit from learning to love whole, nonprocessed foods, and these healthy eating habits should last a lifetime. You may also be surprised to find that making homemade baby food changes the way you think about feeding the rest of the family, too!

Economical Bonus: Believe it or not, you actually save money when you make homemade baby food. And you save not only on the cost of the actual baby food, but in the nutrient ratio as well. You get more nutrient-dense foods per dollar, and your baby gets more nutrients for his growing body.

The Fun and Pride Factor: Making baby food is actually a lot of fun once you find your groove. Shopping for the foods you will be cooking and experimenting with new ingredients is not only rewarding, it's a lot of fun. The results of your culinary efforts will bring you pride and joy when you puree and blend baby food creations, unleashing your inner creative chef for that very special little customer.

Essential Kitchen Ingredients

Before we get started, let's go over some kitchen essentials. These are ingredients to always have on hand for preparing fast, fresh, homemade baby food as well as quick dinners for the whole family. Having just a few of these items from each group will allow you to whip up something tasty and nutritious in no time!

Fruits: apples, avocados, bananas, peaches, pears
Vegetables: carrots, green beans, peas, sweet potatoes, winter
squash (butternut, acorn, hubbard)
Grains: brown rice, oatmeal
Meats and Proteins: chicken breasts, eggs
Other: herbs, spices, plain whole-milk yogurt

Incorporating Baby Food Making into Your Routine

The key to making the homemade baby food process flow smoothly into your already hectic life is to cook in batches, buy extras, and exploit your oven. As you make your shopping list, add an extra pound of carrots, an extra pound of bananas, a few avocados, and an extra pound of sweet potatoes to what you already planned to buy.

Batch cooking and exploiting your oven saves time and

energy—your energy and the energy that powers your oven. Is your oven always packed full of foods to be cooked, or do you typically have one lonely roast in that cavernous space? Stuff your oven full of foods that you will be feeding your baby. When you are making the family dinner, add a few sweet potatoes to bake in the oven. Peel and wrap some carrots in tinfoil with a drizzle of olive oil and place them next to the sweet potatoes. Don't stop there! Cut a few apples in half and place them in a small baking dish with a bit of water and put them in the oven, too. Once you have all these foods cooked, set them aside to cool and then store them in the refrigerator. You can puree them after your meal if you have time, or the next day.

Tools You Will Need to Make Homemade Baby Food

As mentioned earlier, all the tools and gadgets that you will need to prepare fresh, nutritious homemade baby food are probably already in your kitchen. Following is a full list of tools that would be ideal.

Blender and/or Food Processor: You will use this for pureeing, blending, and mashing foods. There is no need to buy a fancy baby food maker, as a blender/food processor can perform many tasks and will give you far more value for the money.

Immersion Blender or Stick Mixer: This wand mixer comes with a few attachments for blending, chopping, and even whisking. Great for whipping up "on the go" meals, the immersion blender or stick mixer can blend your foods directly in the cooking pot. You can use it for pureeing small amounts of foods or creating soups and smoothies for the whole family. It's easy to use and easy to store.

Food Grinder: While this tool does have its advantages, it limits you to grinding foods in small quantities and/or "on the go" meals. However, this limitation makes the food grinder a great choice for taking to a restaurant, because you will be able to grind up fresh food for your baby right at the table. Food grinders are seldom able to create a texture fine enough for those "stage one" baby foods but would be great for chunkier foods.

Ice Cube Trays /Storage Containers for Freezing: If you don't already have ice cube trays, then go out and buy three or four of them to use for freezing food cubes. You can buy regular plastic ice trays, stainless steel ice trays, or even silicone trays. If you want to have some fun, buy silicone trays that come in cute little shapes like hearts and butterflies. I have often thought it would be great if we could just dump baby food purees into the ice maker and then voilà, out pops frozen baby food cubes!

Freezer Bags: Invest in some heavy-duty freezer bags for storing the frozen food cubes you will pop out of the ice trays. You can recycle the bags by washing in warm soapy water and drying on a dish rack.

Strainer/Colander: A strainer or colander is wonderful for holding and draining fruits and vegetables after they have cooked and even for rinsing and cleaning the food.

Small-Holed Strainer/Fine Mesh Strainer: A fine mesh strainer is good for straining more textured foods to make a finer and smoother puree. It's especially useful for separating green bean and pea skins from puree. You can also use it with cheesecloth to make yogurt cheese!

Stainless Steel Steamer Basket: The steamer basket is a must-have and is very inexpensive (usually around $5 at most). It's used for steaming fruits and vegetables, of course, but it can also hold foods that you will be cleaning and rinsing and even steam-cook meats such as dices of chicken or pork.

Masher: Invest in a good potato masher and you won't have any regrets. A potato masher is perfect for mashing vegetables and fruits when baby graduates to a thicker or chunkier texture.

Cheese Grater, Four-Sided: This is very useful for when your baby is moving on to more finger foods and beginning to self-feed. Using a cheese grater, you can grate meats, fruits and veggies...and yes, even cheese!

Sharpie or Permanent Marker: You really need this if you will be freezing your baby foods so that you may label the freezer bags with the food cube type and the date you prepared and froze the food.

Recommended Appliances for Making Homemade Baby Food

Stage One: For the thin, watery purees that make up baby's first solids, use a blender, a good hand/wand/stick mixer, a Vitamix, or a food processor. For best results, select the "liquefy" and/or "puree" settings.

Stage Two: To create the thicker purees required as your baby moves on to more texture, work with a blender, a good hand/wand/stick mixer, a Vitamix, a food processor, a food mill/grinder, a "ricer," or a potato masher. To get a thicker texture, simply adjust the settings on your machine to "blend," "mix," or "puree," then use more of a pulse than a continual whir.

Stage Three: As your little one gets ready to enjoy the textures of your family's meals, use a blender, a Vitamix, a food mill/grinder, a "ricer," a potato masher, or a food processor to create chunky, thick purees and "table foods." If you want a more chunky texture, change the settings on your chosen appliance to "grind," "mix," and/or "chop"; again, you should use more of a pulse than a continual whir.

CHAPTER SIX

Put On Your Chef's Hat, It's Time to Get Cooking!

Now that you have your instruments, tools, and appliances in order, we're almost ready to make tasty, wholesome baby food. While there are a few precautions you should take that will be discussed in further detail, it's good to remember that making baby food is just like preparing and cooking food for big kids and adults. Baby food, after all, is simply grown-up food that is mashed or pureed or chopped. Just remember to pay attention to cleanliness, proper cooking times, and removing skins or peels to avoid choking hazards.

Washing and Scrubbing and Cleaning

Always wash your hands thoroughly before preparing homemade baby foods. Cleanliness is a must, as baby's delicate system is susceptible to germs that may be hiding out. Yes, washing your hands seems obvious and you already knew that; I just wanted to remind you. It's also important to clean all of the kitchen equipment and food preparation areas you use, such as countertops, utensils, pots and pans, cutting boards, and your blender or food processor—clean everything thoroughly, preferably with an antibacterial soap.

Never use the same cutting board to cut meats and fruits and vegetables. You should have a cutting board solely for meat preparation and a cutting board dedicated to vegetable and fruit preparation. Thus far, no clear guidelines have been established by any food safety agencies in the United States as to whether a wooden cutting board is more sanitary than a plastic board. For now, the focus should be on proper sanitization no matter the materials.

Safe Methods of Proper Food Preparation

When you make homemade baby food, you can use the specific methods of preparation and storage I'll discuss here to help keep your baby's food free from food-borne pathogens. These methods are simple and based in common sense, and you may even be using them already. Read on to find out!

Fruits and Vegetables

Always be sure to thoroughly wash and cleanse the fruits and vegetables you will be using to make your baby food. Even if you are not using the peels or skins, and even if you buy organic, you should always wash your produce. There is no need to invest in a "veggie wash." If you prefer, you may use a solution of water and vinegar at 2 tablespoons of vinegar per 1 cup of water; put this in a spray bottle and you have a simple, inexpensive, and effective wash.

Peeling skins and pitting or removing seeds may be important prior to cooking. There are times when you do not need to peel or pit or remove seeds from produce; these instances will vary according to your baby's age, the fruit or vegetable that you are cooking, and the way in which you will be cooking the foods. Pears and peaches, for example, have a very soft and digestible skin that need not be removed if your baby is over seven months old. Apples have a tougher skin and may not be easily digested by babies under eight months of age. There should be no need to remove the seeds from blueberries; however, it is necessary to seed melons and cucumbers. Consult with your pediatrician about the need to peel fruits and vegetables when making homemade baby foods.

Meat, Poultry, Fish, or Animal Protein

When you are preparing and/or handling meats, it is important that you sanitize your hands as you cook. (It is also a good sanitary practice to use plastic gloves when handling meats.) If you are going back and forth from preparing meats to preparing another type of food, be sure to wash your hands prior to handling the other food. This is most important when you are handling poultry products, including eggs, because of the risk of salmonella.

- In cooking, do not reuse the preparation surfaces or utensils that you have been using to prepare meats without sanitizing them first.
- Meat should always be thawed in the refrigerator. You may use the microwave to thaw meat if you wish, but never leave meat out on the counter to thaw. Thawing food on the counter increases the risk of bacterial growth and may put you at risk for food poisoning.

- Never give an infant raw, rare, or semicooked meat, poultry, fish, and eggs. In other words, babies and even toddlers need their meats cooked to well done. Meats that you are cooking for babies, toddlers, and even older children should not have a pink center.
- Be sure to check the temperature with a meat thermometer whenever possible.

Safe Internal Temperatures for Cooked Meats

Red Meat	Poultry	Eggs	Fish
160° F	white meat—170° F	No runny whites or runny yolks	160° F
	dark meat—180° F	Hard-boiled eggs spin, but raw eggs do not	

Other Food Safety Tips

- Do not leave uncooked or even cooked foods out on the counter at room temperature for longer than two hours.
- Frozen foods should never thaw and then be refrozen without first being cooked. For optimal safety and nutrient retention, frozen foods should remain at a temperature of 0 degrees or lower. Temperature fluctuations within the freezer, such as occur when you open the door to rummage around for something, can affect the stability of frozen foods. Try not to store frozen baby food cubes on the freezer door. As far back into the freezer as possible is best.
- Cooked and prepared foods should be kept in the refrigerator for no longer than forty-eight to seventy-two hours before they are used or frozen. Yes, my husband

has eaten that container of "who-knows-what" from the back of the fridge and has survived, but really, this is not a good idea!

- Foods in the freezer will have varying storage times depending on how they were prepared prior to freezing. It is prudent to use frozen baby food cubes within one month, though they may be stored for up to three months in a regular freezer and six months in a deep freezer, where the temperature is lower and more constant.

Ingredients and Preparation of Foods— Choose Organic Foods When Possible!

As a parent, you may be wondering if it really makes a difference whether or not you use organic products to make homemade baby food. Some people may tell you that you should use only organic foods when cooking for your baby, while

Did you know that foods imported from other countries may contain higher levels of synthetic pesticides—even synthetic pesticides that are banned in the United States? Whenever possible, purchase fruits and vegetables that are grown in the United States. If you are outside the United States, check with your country's agricultural agencies and ask about the policy on imported foods and the use of pesticides.

others may tell you that using conventional foods or a mix of both is perfectly acceptable. Ultimately, this is a personal choice. Many people "go organic" because they want to know that their foods are free from pesticides and chemical fertilizers. A few other factors may also influence your decision to purchase organic foods: lifestyle, accessibility, and price, for instance. Buying and preparing organic foods for your baby will have great health advantages, and if you are able to buy only a few items that are organic, make those the ones that you feed to your little one. Babies who eat organic foods will not be exposed to the levels of pesticides found in conventional foods, and you can ensure that baby's tiny system remains as free of chemicals as possible. It is said that pound for pound, a baby consumes more pesticides than an adult because of his small body size, and pound for pound, a baby eats more fruits and vegetables than an adult.

Many parents use organic foods just to prepare their baby's meals, while other parents have never bought organic foods for their babies. If you don't have access to or cannot afford the price of organic food, it is still worth using fresh conventional fruits and vegetables to make your baby food, as simply making your own baby food has so many benefits.

Don't let people tell you that you are wasting your time if you don't use organic foods. Don't let this stop you from cooking up wholesome baby food. Using fresh, well-cleansed non-organic fruits, vegetables, and whole grains is completely suitable and remains a healthy and nutritious choice for making your baby's food. Just remember that you are feeding your baby fresh foods, developing healthy eating habits very early on, and giving your baby more nutritional value per ounce than if you were to feed him jarred foods.

According to the Environmental Working Group (EWG), a

nonprofit agency that works to protect citizens from chemicals in food, water, and common everyday products, there are at least twelve foods that you should always buy organic if possible: the "dirty dozen." The EWG also tracks the fifteen foods that are found to be the least contaminated by pesticides, fertilizers, or other chemicals.

EWG's 2011 Dirty Dozen and Clean Fifteen Produce List

Twelve Most Contaminated	Fifteen Least Contaminated
Buy organic when possible:	Safe non-organic choices:
Apples	Asparagus
Bell peppers	Avocados
Blueberries	Cabbage
Celery	Cantaloupe (domestic)
Grapes, esp. imported	Eggplants
Kale	Grapefruit
Lettuce	Kiwi
Nectarines	Mangoes
Peaches	Mushrooms
Potatoes	Onions
Spinach	Pineapples
Strawberries	Sweet corn
	Sweet peas
	Sweet potatoes
	Watermelons

Preparing Fruits and Vegetables

Preparing fruits and vegetables for babies is as simple as preparing them for adults but there are a few extra considerations such as whether or not to peel or cook them. The toughness of the skin or peel, whether or not the "meat" of the fruit or vegetable can be chewed and easily digested raw, and your baby's age will all be deciding factors.

Is it necessary to peel fruits and veggies before preparing them for baby food?

We know that the peels or skins of many fruits and vegetables contain valuable nutrients. For adults, whenever possible leave the peels and skins on fruits and vegetables to allow you to take full advantage of the nutrients found in them. However, if you are preparing baby food, it may be a good idea to take off the peels and skins for a few reasons.

Perhaps the most important advantage is that it may help to stave off digestive upsets. All babies are different, of course; some will be able to tolerate the peels without any difficulty, but others won't. While some nutrients may be lost when you peel fruits and/or vegetables, the loss will not be significant—and you'll be able to avoid the possibility that baby may choke on a piece of peel floating in the puree.

Another good reason to peel fruits and vegetables is that it will help decrease pesticide residue. Of course, some veggies and fruits, like acorn squash and avocado, have an inedible peel that has to be removed.

Use your own judgment and/or contact your pediatrician about leaving the peels and skins on the foods you will be preparing.

Is it necessary to cook fruits and vegetables when making homemade baby food?

You will find that many pediatricians who endorse making baby food will also recommend cooking fruits until baby is about seven to eight months old. Depending on the doctor, this age recommendation may vary. And some doctors may say cooking fruits is not necessary at all. Bananas and avocado are the key exception (and some say that peaches and pears are also exceptions), in that these fruits need never be cooked. For infants who start solids before six months of age, cooking fruits is best, because the process gently breaks down the fibers and sugars and eases digestion for an immature tummy. An older baby may be better able to handle raw fruits than one who is younger and just starting on solids. While there are no immediate life-threatening health risks to feeding a baby raw fruits, if your baby experiences some digestion and tummy troubles, continue to gently cook raw fruits for another week or two. Tummy troubles and digestive upsets from raw fruits should go away once the fruit itself has been passed.

Using Frozen and/or Canned Foods

One question that is commonly asked about making homemade baby food is: "Can I use frozen or canned ingredients to make baby food?" The answer is this: Fresh foods, particularly those that are also local and in season are a great first choice, but frozen foods are fine as well. Canned foods, while convenient, have a lot of down sides, which I'll explain here.

Is it safe to use frozen foods to make homemade baby food?

Frozen fruits and vegetables are sometimes a better alternative than fresh foods when making homemade baby food. In fact, many food safety resources and authorities say that frozen foods can be more "fresh" than fresh. Fresh foods may spend weeks traveling around the country until they arrive at your grocer's, and this can affect their overall quality (a good reason to buy local foods whenever possible). Picked at the peak of ripeness, many fruits and vegetables are flash-frozen directly at the place of harvest. Flash-freezing protects the nutritional quality of the foods, enabling them to withstand long journeys without impacting the quality. When seasonal fruits and vegetables are unavailable fresh at the market, using frozen is perfectly acceptable—and certainly much better than canned!

When selecting frozen fruits or vegetables, be sure to read the labels and avoid brands that contain syrups, sugars, and salt or sodium. A few types of frozen vegetables have been previously cooked and then frozen; avoid using these, as you should not cook, freeze, and then cook and refreeze foods.

Freezing Foods Rule:
Foods that are not cooked (raw) may be frozen and then thawed, cooked, and refrozen. Once you have thawed the cooked food, you should never refreeze any leftovers.

Using canned food to make baby food is not a good option.

Using canned foods to make homemade baby food may be safe, but it's not really the best choice. In the canning process, foods are often cooked at high temperatures and the can is then filled with liquid (syrup or brine). Once the can has been filled, it may be heated again before the final sterilization, during which the can and its contents are cooked at a temperature high enough to ensure a long shelf life.

One problem with this process is that the nutrients in the food may be severely depleted, and further cooking, freezing, and reheating the foods may lead to an additional loss of precious nutrients. Canned foods also sit around for months on a shelf, and many of their nutrients leach into the water in which they are packed. When we open canned foods, we often toss out the packing liquid, thereby tossing out some nutrients as well. It is possible to use the liquids that the food was canned in to make a baby food puree, but these liquids typically contain high amounts of sodium; even canned foods that are "low-sodium" are not appropriate to serve to infants.

Another negative is that many of the cans are lined with a coating that contains BPA (bisphenol A), and the BPA may leach into the foods when they are heated. Finally, canned fruits and vegetables will have a texture that is very soft and often mushy. While this may be good for finger foods, purees made from canned food will be very runny and a bit grainy.

If you are making your baby's food from scratch, you will want her to fall in love with the tastes and textures of fresh foods. Using canned foods will not help you achieve this goal.

*   *   *

Time-saver: You may use canned pumpkin when making pumpkin baby food. Please make sure that you purchase canned pure pumpkin and not a "pumpkin pie" mix. The pumpkin pie mix contains sugars, starches, and other additives. I do not generally recommend using canned foods for baby's homemade food, but canned pumpkin is a great alternative, as it contains nothing but pumpkin!

CHAPTER SEVEN

Creating Tasty Homemade Baby Foods

This chapter will outline the simple and almost effort-less methods of cooking, preparing, storing, and even heating and serving homemade baby food. Making baby food is as easy as baking or steaming food and then pureeing and storing it for future feedings. The basic methods outlined are used for all types of foods and recipes that you will turn into fresh and tasty homemade baby foods!

Methods for Cooking the Food

Cooking the foods that you have chosen to make for your baby is the first step in making homemade baby food. You may steam, bake, microwave, or boil the foods in a scant amount of water. Steaming and baking will help to maintain the most nutrients and allow you to whip up large batches of foods at one time. Big-batch cooking is a time-saver, and "exploiting your oven" whenever possible is highly recommended.

Salt and sugar are never needed when making baby food. Tasty spices and herbs such as nutmeg, cinnamon, ginger, basil, tarragon, garlic powder, pepper, and the like may be introduced as early as seven months with your pediatrician's consent.

You may also use a microwave to cook your baby's foods if you plan to puree and store only a small amount to use for a few days at a time. Remember that it is always best to microwave foods in glass containers, not in plastic. Research indicates that plastic may leach chemicals when heated. Many parents prefer not to use a microwave (I am not a big fan of cooking this way), and I suggest that you make steaming or baking the preferred method of cooking foods for baby.

There's gold in that liquid! Be sure to set aside the liquid that the vegetable/fruits were cooked in because it contains a wealth of nutrients. (Do not use reserved water from carrots or other high-nitrate veggies for a baby under seven months old. Read more about nitrates on page 54.) You may also thin homemade baby food with formula, breast milk (not previously frozen breast milk if you will be freezing the baby food), plain water, or a splash of natural fruit juice; the choice is yours.

Pureeing the Food

Once foods are cooked and have cooled a bit, add them in small increments to the machine you have decided to use for pureeing. Use the cooking liquids you have set aside to create a thin puree. Remember that this liquid helps to return any nutrients that may have leached into the water during cooking.

For any type of machine you may use to puree, the secret to fewer lumps and bumps lies in how much food you put in the container baskets to begin with. No appliance will do a good job of pureeing or blending uniformly if it's overstuffed. Fill the containers less than half-full and add a scant amount of liquid to begin.

Set your machine to puree or grind or chop and then process the vegetables or fruits. As you are pureeing or blending the food, slowly add the liquid you have decided to use.

Thinning the Puree

Using breast milk or formula to thin the foods gives them a nutritional boost and adds a familiar taste for baby. But if you plan to thin your baby food first and then freeze it for later use, bear in mind the following regarding each of these liquids as thinners: First, if you want to thin with *breast milk*, do not use any that was previously frozen; the process of thawing and refreezing breast milk depletes its nutritional properties. Second, while it's fine to freeze the baby puree you make using *formula* as a thinner, the formula by itself must never be frozen, not in bottles or cans (whether you've mixed it yourself or bought the pre-mixed type); as the formula companies note, this causes a separation of the fats from the liquid and the texture (and quality) will suffer.

Many parents who freeze their baby food prefer not to thin it until later, after they have thawed whatever amount they wish to use. Thinning the foods right before they will be served to your little one allows you to use any liquid you wish. (Of course, pureeing baby's foods without adding any liquids at all is also a fine option.)

Thickening the Puree

There may be times when the puree you have made is too thin and runny or the foods thaw to a thin or runny texture. If you want to thicken the puree, consider adding commercial baby cereal, yogurt, cooked rice or oatmeal, or even another fruit or vegetable such as banana or sweet potato. There are no "rules" as to how thick or how thin your purees should be; let your baby's age and stage be your guide.

Storing Homemade Baby Food Puree in the Refrigerator

If you would like to store your homemade baby food in the refrigerator, use an airtight plastic or glass container. Many pediatricians and health and food safety experts recommend refrigerating fresh pureed homemade baby food no longer than forty-eight hours (many food safety authorities say that seventy-two hours is fine). This ensures that bacteria growth in the puree is kept to a minimum and that the food does not take on the "taste of the fridge" (a stale or "off" taste and smell that comes from sitting too long in the refrigerator).

If you do not plan to freeze your homemade pureed baby food, try to make the purees on a daily, or every-other-day, basis to ensure top quality. To simplify this process, cook in batches and freeze in unpureed portions. For example, you could bake one sweet potato and then freeze one half without pureeing it.

Puree the other half of the sweet potato for two days' worth of meals. This will help cut down on waste and allow you to maintain quality and food safety. If you do make small batches and store in the refrigerator, do not feed your baby from the container and then re-store. Saliva may contaminate the food and bacteria may evolve. Always take the portions you will serve from the container and transfer to a feeding bowl.

There is a drawback to making homemade baby food on a daily/every-other-day basis: If you are just beginning to introduce solid foods, you will not be able to determine if your baby has a true dislike for a food until much later. This could lead to wasted food. Experts say that it takes an infant between fifteen and twenty-one instances of trying a food before a true like or dislike is established. When you use the freezer method for storing purees, you will be able to try a rejected food over (and over) again without having to make and possibly waste the same food again.

Storing Homemade Baby Food Puree in the Freezer

Once you have a nice thin baby food puree that is acceptable to your baby, you will then transfer the puree into ice cube trays for freezing/storage. Fill each cube with the puree, as though you were filling the tray with water to make ice cubes.

Cover the tray tightly with plastic wrap (foil is not recommended, as shards of the foil may be left on/in the food cubes) and put it in the freezer. Repeat this process until you have filled all the trays and no puree remains. Tupperware and OXO are two brands that make great ice cube trays that come with lids (if you would prefer getting trays with lids). Prices typically range from $4 to $7 per set.

Frozen baby food cubes should be used within a month of freezing for optimal nutrient retention. You may store the food cubes for as long as three months if you need to, in a regular freezer, and up to six months in a deep freezer.

Parents have often asked me about the safety of freezing baby food in recycled glass jars rather than in ice cube trays. I always reply that you should *never freeze foods in glass not labeled for freezing*! Apologies for "screaming" out this warning, but it is very important that you do not freeze your homemade baby foods in glass containers that are not labeled safe for freezing. Glass that is not manufactured specifically for freezing could crack, leave behind microscopic shards or fragments, or even burst. Many people do freeze their homemade baby food in recycled baby food jars and have not had any issues, but that does not mean the process is safe. Commercial baby food companies do not recommend freezing the glass, nor do they recommend freezing the plastic containers. Neither type of container has been manufactured to withstand extreme fluctuations in temperature. You're making baby's food so he can have the best nutrition possible; why take a risk by freezing his foods in jars? If you prefer to freeze homemade baby food in glass, please use jars that are manufactured specifically for freezing.

Once the cubes of puree have set and are frozen, remove the trays from the freezer and transfer the cubes into freezer bags. Using a Sharpie or other type of permanent marker, label the freezer bag with the date of preparation as well as the type of food. Labeling is essential, because in this form you will not be able to distinguish between carrots and sweet potatoes or between green beans and peas. When it is time to feed baby, you simply take out the number of food cubes needed, thaw, and reheat.

Freezing baby food purees is the most recommended method of storage to ensure optimal food safety (and convenience). Even parents who strictly follow the four-day-wait rule and

Helpful hint: Each baby food cube is equal to approximately 1 ounce of food, and there are approximately 2 tablespoons per ounce.

feed only one type of food at a time find it easier to cook and freeze in bulk than to cook every few days.

Baby food cubes may safely remain in the freezer from three to six months, but using them within one to three months is most prudent. Owing to the amount of water crystals that tend to build up on baby food purees, causing nutrients to leach or evaporate upon thawing, it is best to use your frozen baby foods cubes as soon as possible. Many food safety experts such as those at Clemson University and agencies like the FDA and USDA issue guidelines that note that most fruits and veggies will keep from eight to twelve months in the freezer, but these guidelines are for fruits and vegetables that have not been cooked and turned into purees. If you're interested in seeing them anyway, see page 306 of Appendix IV for details on where to find them. Moreover, such recommendations assume that the freezer remains at a constant subzero temperature. Be sure to put homemade baby food in the back of the freezer for optimal quality; anything stored in the door of the freezer may be subject to temperature fluctuations each time the door is opened. Storing foods in a deep freezer is best should you wish to keep them for a long period of time.

Don't be alarmed if you see ice crystals on your baby food

cubes. Ice crystals will form as the excess liquid used to make the puree rises and freezes at the tops of the cubes. These crystals are often mistaken for freezer burn, but their presence is not dangerous and will not make the foods inedible.

> Crystals on frozen baby foods are not freezer burn but a result of excess liquids being frozen. Freezer burn looks like grayish brown spots on the frozen item. It appears as a leathery-type texture and is easily noticeable.
>
>

When should the puree be stored?

While the professional food safety jury is still divided, here is the most highly recommended food safety advice on storing foods:

Refrigerate or freeze perishable foods promptly. Harmful bacteria can grow rapidly if foods aren't properly cooled. It is important to store perishable foods within two hours of purchasing or preparing them. If the room temperature is above 90 degrees, refrigerate perishable foods within one hour. Freeze ground meat, poultry, fish, and shellfish if you don't expect to eat it within two days, and freeze beef, veal, lamb, or pork within three to five days.

Some say that immediately transferring *hot* foods to the freezer is *not* good because it will affect the temperature of the foods around it and possibly the temperature of the whole freezer. I recommend transferring cooked food to the fridge and then packaging it for freezer storage within two to three hours. You may safely leave prepared foods in the fridge for up to forty-eight hours (seventy-two hours *max*), so it is up to you whether you want to immediately move your foods to the freezer. If you decide to leave the food in the refrigerator for a few days before freezing it, make a note that you have food in the refrigerator that needs to be frozen. There have been a few times that I have forgotten about the food I needed to transfer to the freezer, and sadly, I could not offer it to my babies. If this happens to you, all is not lost, as you should be able to find some use for the food: toss it into a pasta sauce or a smoothie, for example.

So You're Ready to Eat?

There are several ways to safely thaw and heat homemade baby food, which we'll talk about here. The method that you choose is entirely up to you, but please test the temperature of any food you will be serving to your baby so that baby does not accidentally burn her mouth or tongue!

Microwave Thawing and Heating

Using the microwave to thaw and/or heat baby food is by far the fastest and simplest method. Take out the amount of food needed and place it into a bowl. Always thaw and warm baby food cubes in a glass bowl rather than in plastic containers, as research indicates heating glass in the microwave is safer. Heat the food in small intervals so that you have better control over the temperature, and be sure to stir the food well in between to avoid any hot pockets that might burn your baby. Many parents do not like to use the microwave for a variety of reasons; it's up to you to decide what is right for you and your baby.

Do not feed your baby from the food container and then reuse the container or food that baby has been fed from. Saliva may contaminate the food, and bacteria may evolve. Always take the portions you will serve from the container and transfer to a feeding bowl.

Refrigerator Thawing

If you do not wish to use a microwave to thaw your baby food cubes, thawing the baby food cubes in the refrigerator overnight is a good option. Thawing in the refrigerator may take up to twelve hours, so be sure to plan accordingly; for example, you might wish to take the food cubes out of the freezer and put them in the refrigerator one day in advance of planned meals. Be sure that the cubes are kept in a closed container and not in an uncovered bowl.

Submersion or Warm Water Thawing

Another great way to thaw and even heat homemade baby food is to place the cubes in a small bowl and then place that bowl in a larger vessel filled with hot water. This "submersion" or "floating" method should take anywhere from ten to twenty minutes. You can also do this with a pan of warm water on the stove. Just add the smaller (use glass) bowl to a pot of water that you have warmed; this is basically the same as using a double boiler.

Stovetop Thawing and Heating

Stovetop thawing is similar to the submersion method (and it too works on the principle of the double boiler). Fill a medium-sized saucepan about half-full with water and bring to a boil. Turn down the heat and gently add the bowl of cubes. (You could also add a steamer basket to the pan and place the bowl of cubes in the basket.) The stovetop method will thaw the cubes in ten to twenty minutes.

Bear in mind that you do not have to serve baby food hot, nor is it necessary to fully heat your thawing baby food cubes; it depends on your child's preferences. Thawing food in any of the methods described above and then serving it room temperature is fine; in fact, many babies prefer foods served at room temperature. (Note, however, that thawing food on your kitchen counter is not recommended, as bacteria or other contaminants may get into the food.)

Packing and Traveling with Homemade Baby Food—You Can Take It with You When You Go!

Homemade baby food is easy to take with you wherever you may roam. Sure, those jars might be more convenient to toss into a diaper bag or suitcase, but with a bit of planning, you and your baby can even go on a six-day camping trip five hours away without access to a refrigerator and still have homemade baby food! (Call me crazy, but I took my infant twins on a camping trip—and it actually worked quite well!)

Here are the basics. Buy a small soft-sided mini-cooler and first toss in the "traveling trio," as I like to call it: a fork, a bowl with a lid, and a banana or an avocado. You'll be able to mash at will whenever your little one gets hungry. The traveling trio is useful for day trips, for plane travel, and for when you venture back into the world of dining out. You can even take a small mini–food grinder/mill with you.

For trips that require days away from home, here are a few ideas to consider: Take along a mini-cooler packed full of the frozen food cubes you will need (this will require you to plot out how many cubes of each particular food you will feed to your baby during the time you'll be away from home). If you've been using the freezer bag storage method, simply take out each freezer bag of food cubes and arrange in the cooler with ice packs. Since the cubes are already frozen, they should be able to withstand a journey of six hours with minimal thawing. You can also take your cubes to a hotel, as many now provide mini-refrigerators. If you have packed a large number of cubes, they should keep for approximately four to five days if stored in a refrigerator as they slowly thaw out. Be sure to start with the cubes that have thawed the most—you don't want to use food that has been thawed for more than seventy-two hours.

You can heat and/or thaw the food just as you do at home if appliances are available, or you may thaw and heat over a gas stove or campfire via the submersion method. And don't forget, you can always buy fresh fruits in the local grocery stores wherever you might be staying.

If you feel that toting your homemade baby food when out and about is too difficult, don't hesitate to pack jars of commercial baby food and boxes of commercial cereal. But if you decide to go this route, I suggest serving your baby some commercial baby foods a week or so prior to your journey. There are babies who will refuse to eat commercial baby foods, especially if they have been brought up thus far only on homemade baby food.

PART II

Homemade Baby Food—
Recipes and Tips for Feeding Your Baby with Wholesome Goodness and Love!

*W*elcome to the recipe section of *The Wholesome Baby Food Guide*. This is really the heart and soul of the book because here is where you will find all sorts of amazingly easy and totally delicious recipes. Many of these recipes for homemade baby food, including foods and meals that the whole family can enjoy together, have been made and tested for over seven years by the millions of visitors to the Wholesome Baby Food website (wholesomebabyfood.com). In this book, you will find more than fifty exclusive recipes. As the website has evolved and I have been able to expand my culinary adventures as my boys get older, I find myself continuing to see that most of the dishes I now prepare are easily converted to fresh and easy recipes and meals that babies will be able to enjoy. Sometimes even I forget about the best-kept secret of all types of baby food: it is nothing more than adult food that has been mashed or pureed!

The recipes in this book use readily available ingredients, and every effort is made to ensure that the instructions are easy to follow, with limited steps and commentary to clutter up the recipe and confuse the chef.

We all know how difficult it is to take care of a baby while trying to cook up tasty meals for the whole family. This is why you'll find foods and recipes that the whole family will be able to enjoy!

Four to Six Months of Age— Tasty Recipes for Stage One Beginners

---

CEREALS & GRAINS: Barley, Oat, Rice
FRUITS: Apples, Avocados, Bananas, Pears
VEGETABLES: Acorn/Butternut Squash, Green Beans,
    Sweet Potatoes
PROTEIN: None
DAIRY: None

The recipes that follow are ideal for babies who are beginning their solid food adventures between four and six months of age. While many pediatric resources recommend beginning solids at six months, introducing baby to the world of solid foods at four months is entirely acceptable. As always, be sure to consult your baby's pediatrician about introducing solid foods between four and six months of age and be sure to review the first chapter in part I of this book for more information. If your baby was born prematurely, it is a good idea to double-check with your pediatrician about the best age to start solid foods. The generally accepted practice is to use a baby's corrected or adjusted age.

Remember that between the ages of four and six months, breast milk and/or formula will be the most important source of nutrition for your baby. Do not replace baby's milk with solids until your pediatrician indicates this is appropriate for your baby!

Relaxing the four-day-wait rule to two or three days is acceptable (see page 13), but remember: your baby is just starting solid foods and there is no need to rush things.

As you read through these deliciously fresh recipes, you will notice that most of the stage one and stage two meals do not indicate serving or portion size. It is my experience that the yield from these recipes depends entirely on the person doing the cooking and pureeing. I can manage to get almost two full ice trays from one large sweet potato, while others might get only half a tray. The reason for such variance in serving yield is that if I add more water, I will get more servings. If you add less water and puree for less time, you will get fewer servings. If I cook a larger sweet potato and am able to scoop out more "meat" from it, I will also get a larger yield.

Enjoy these delicious, tasty, and simple first foods recipes.

Stage One Sample Meal Plan—Beginners

Exact portion size is not shown because not all babies will be eating the same amounts of solid foods. Begin with smaller portions (1 to 2 tablespoons) and then slowly work your way up as your baby shows signs of being ready for more. In this stage, consider offering meals in the late morning and again in the early afternoon if desired. Remember, breast milk and/or formula will be your baby's main nutrition at this stage; don't allow solids to take up too much tummy room.

Early Morning Waking: Breast milk and/or formula

Meal	Monday	Tuesday	Wednesday	Thursday	Friday	Saturday	Sunday
8:00–9:00 a.m. Breakfast—1 to 3 tablespoons	sweet potatoes	sweet potatoes	sweet potatoes	avocado	avocado	avocado	oatmeal

Midmorning: Breast milk and/or formula

| 12:00–1:00 p.m. Lunch—1 to 3 tablespoons | breast milk and/or formula | breast milk and/or formula | breast milk and/or formula | breast milk and/or formula | breast milk and/or formula | breast milk and/or formula | breast milk and/or formula |

Midafternoon: Breast milk and/or formula

| 4:00–5:00 p.m. Dinner—1 to 3 tablespoons | breast milk and/or formula | breast milk and/or formula | breast milk and/or formula | breast milk and/or formula | breast milk and/or formula | breast milk and/or formula | breast milk and/or formula |

Before Bedtime: Breast milk and/or formula

FRUITS

Amazing Applesauce

Tools: vegetable peeler, sharp knife, saucepan, potato masher and/or whisk, blender or food processor (optional)

Apples (any amount you desire; try using 5 to 10 large apples such as Fuji, Macintosh, Gala, or Braeburn)

Peel, core, and cut apples into slices or chunks. Place the apples into a saucepan that contains just enough water to slightly cover the slices, then bring the water to a boil and steam the slices until tender, approximately 15 minutes. Be sure to check on the water level and stir periodically.

Place slices into a bowl and reserve any leftover water. Apples may be mashed with a potato masher or pureed if needed. Add the reserved water as necessary to achieve a smooth, thin puree.

Freezes with mixed results: Some browning may occur; try a drip of lemon juice in the puree prior to freezing.

Quick Tip: Select apples that are firm and without squishy indentations. Apple skin should not be discolored (uneven coloring is the hallmark of many apples, so do not mistake discoloration for normal coloring) or have cuts and bruises.

Did You Know?

Apples are great fruits for maintaining bowel regularity because of their insoluble and soluble fiber content. Unfortunately, applesauce may constipate babies who are just starting out on solid foods. So be sure to offer applesauce in moderation!

> *Quick Tip:* Save the cooking juice and freeze in ice trays for homemade apple juice. Use juice cubes to help with constipation or to add flavor to baby's other foods.

Awesome Avocado

Tools: sharp knife, fork, blender or food processor (optional)

1 ripe Haas avocado

To remove avocado pit, slice avocado in half around the pit, twist the two halves to open, and scoop the pit out. Scoop out meat from shell into a bowl. Mash avocado meat with a fork until smooth and creamy. (You may also puree the avocado in a blender or food processor if desired.)

Freezes with mixed results: Some browning may occur, and texture may suffer.

Did You Know?

A ripe avocado will be soft to the touch, and when cut open, it will be a creamy green color that slowly transforms into a light yellow buttery color.

Quick Tip: You can freeze avocados in slices. Simply peel, pit, and then slice the avocados. You may use a lemon bath or freeze the slices naked. Lay them on a cookie sheet or tray and place in freezer. Once frozen, transfer the slices to a freezer bag.

Lemon Bath: Create a bath of ½ cup water and 2 squeeze-drips of lemon juice. Bathe the slices in the mixture prior to freezing. This will help retard browning.

Thaw as many slices as you wish, then mash and serve to your baby.

Banana-Rama

Tools: sharp knife, fork, blender or food processor (optional)

1 ripe banana
Formula, breast milk, or water

Peel the banana and break it into small pieces in a bowl. Mash the pieces with a fork, using a whisking motion until the banana is smooth and creamy. Add formula, breast milk, or water if needed to create a thinner consistency.

(You may also puree the banana in a blender or food processor if desired.)

Freezes with mixed results: Some browning may occur; try a drip of lemon juice in the puree prior to freezing.

Did You Know?

Bananas can be frozen right in their jackets/peel; simply wrap in plastic wrap, place in a freezer bag, and freeze for up to six months. Bananas are known to cause constipation, so be sure not to overdo it!

Quick Tip: Using a banana with "sugar spots" will give you a smooth and delicious-tasting banana puree.

A sugar-spotted banana is one that has a bit of brown on the peel with some slight spotting—the point where it is just a few days until you must toss the banana or make banana bread or smoothies.

Peary Perfect Pears

Tools: sharp knife, saucepan, fork, blender or food processor (optional)

6 ripe pears (Bartlett or Anjou)

Peel and deseed the pears. Place pears in a saucepan with about 1 inch of water and steam until the pears are soft and have turned mushy. (About 10 minutes.) Allow pears to cool, then transfer to a bowl and mash with a fork (or puree if needed), using the leftover steaming water to thin if necessary.

Freezes with mixed results: Some browning may occur; try a drip of lemon juice in the puree prior to freezing.

Quick Tip: While pears may be soft and juicy without cooking them and the skin may be blended easily, it is recommended that you cook and peel fruits for babies who are just starting solid foods.

You may add baby cereal to the pear puree if it is too watery.

Did You Know?
Pears are naturally watery and juicy, so you may not need to add extra liquid to thin them. Pears, and even pear juice, are a great fruit to offer as a remedy to alleviate baby's constipation.

Baked Pears

Tools: sharp knife, baking dish, fork, blender or food processor (optional)

6 ripe pears (Bartlett or Anjou)

Preheat the oven to 350 degrees.

Halve and core the pears, then place in a shallow baking dish, flesh side up, with about 1 inch of water. Bake for 25 minutes or until tender. Allow pears to cool, then place in a bowl and mash with a fork (or puree if needed), using the leftover baking water to thin if necessary.

Freezes with mixed results: You can freeze the baked pear halves without mashing or pureeing if you prefer.

Quick Tip: For older babies and kids of all ages, serve warm baked pears with a scoop of frozen or regular yogurt. Mash together if needed.

Baked pears mix nicely into oatmeal, cereal, yogurt, or even chicken.

Pears are amazingly tasty when they are baked; try the Baked Pear Crumble recipe on page 192.

Did You Know?
Baked pears make great finger food and are wonderful for babies who may have sore gums from teething. The soft, tender texture of baked pears (and all baked fruits) means less stress and demand for mashing against sore gums.

Saucy Avocado

Tools: sharp knife, saucepan, potato masher or fork, blender or food processor (optional)

Scooped out meat from ½ a pitted avocado
¼ cup applesauce (homemade or natural)

Mash the avocado, then mix the mashed avocado with applesauce and serve.

Freezes well: This mix may be watery upon thawing, and some browning may occur.

> *Quick Tip:* It is perfectly fine to use a jar of natural applesauce to save you time.
>
>   Read the labels to ensure that the only ingredients are apples and water (citric acid or ascorbic acid as an ingredient is fine, as this form of vitamin C acts as a preservative).

Did You Know?
Applesauce and avocado mashed together makes a great spread for toast or bagels and is tasty even when mixed into yogurt!

Banana 'Cado

Tools: sharp knife, potato masher or fork, blender or food processor (optional)

Scooped out meat from ½ a pitted avocado
½ peeled banana

Mash the avocado, then mash in the banana. Blend thoroughly and serve.

Does not freeze well: For best results, keep this mix in the refrigerator in a tightly sealed container, as browning occurs and texture changes dramatically.

Did You Know?
This recipe has been a favorite on the Wholesome Baby Food website for years! It's easy to prepare and highly nutritious, and babies love it! Try spreading some on toast or whole-grain crackers for a tasty snack for the whole family.

Quick Tip: Bananas and avocados are known to brown rather quickly. This browning (known as oxidization) is normal.

Add a drip of lemon juice to the finished dish and then stir again for a minute prior to serving or storing in the refrigerator.

Peary Apples

Tools: sharp knife, saucepan, potato masher or fork, blender or food processor (optional)

3 apples (Gala, Macintosh, or Braeburn), cored and peeled
3 pears (Bartlett or Anjou), cored and peeled

Dice apples and pears and place in a saucepan with a scant amount of water. Simmer until tender, approximately 10 minutes. Let cool, then mash or puree as needed.

Freezes with mixed results: Puree may be watery upon thawing, and some browning may occur.

Did You Know?
Apples and pears contain a lot of vitamin A, folate, and even calcium.

Quick Tip: Applesauce may be binding and could cause constipation; the addition of pears makes this yummy recipe friendlier to baby's bowels.

Peeling the skin of apples is a good idea for babies who are just beginning solid foods.

VEGETABLES

Butternut Baby

Tools: sharp knife, saucepan or baking dish, large spoon, blender or food processor

1 butternut squash, approximately 2 to 3 pounds

Baking

Preheat the oven to 400 degrees.

Cut squash in half, scoop out seeds. Place halves facedown in a baking dish and cover with 1 inch of water. Bake at 400 degrees for 40 minutes to 1 hour (be sure the "shell/skin" puckers and the halves feel soft). Let cool, then scoop squash "meat" out of the shell, place into blender or food processor, and begin pureeing, adding water as necessary to achieve a smooth, thin consistency.

Boiling or Steaming

Peel washed squash and cut into small chunks. Place chunks into a saucepan with just enough water to slightly cover. (You may use a steamer basket insert if preferred.) Steam or lightly boil the squash until fork tender; be sure to check on the water level. Reserve any leftover water to use for thinning the puree and let the squash cool. Add the squash to a blender or food processor and puree to a consistency that your baby will enjoy.

Freezes well: Puree may be slightly watery upon thawing.

Did You Know?
Butternut and other winter squash varieties are supernutritious, containing over 7,000 mg of vitamin A, and lots of calcium, folate, and even vitamin C. Butternut is also lightly sweet and nutty tasting and is typically a favorite food for most babies.

Quick Tip: To easily cut a butternut or other winter squash, put the whole squash in the microwave for 25 to 30 seconds to soften it up a bit.

When separating the squash meat from the shell, do not scrape too close to the shell or you may find long hard fibers in your squash!

Sweets for My Sweetie

Tools: fork, tinfoil (optional), steamer basket (optional), blender or food processor

   3 medium sweet potatoes

Baking

Preheat oven to 400 degrees.

Wash the sweet potatoes, then poke holes in them using a regular fork (do not peel). Wrap the potatoes in tinfoil if desired. (Sweet potatoes may be baked without being wrapped in foil, though they may take a bit longer to cook.) Place prepared sweet potatoes in the oven and bake at 400 degrees for 30 to 60 minutes. Sweet potato skin will pucker a bit and the potato will be soft and squishy when lightly squeezed. Allow to cool a bit and then slit the potatoes lengthwise and scoop or simply squeeze out the "meat"; discard the skins. Use water, formula, or breast milk to puree or thin the sweet potatoes.

Boiling or Steaming

Peel the washed sweet potatoes and cut them into small chunks. Place the chunks into a saucepan with just enough water to slightly cover. (You may use a steamer basket insert if you have one.) Steam or lightly boil the sweet potatoes until they are fork tender; be sure to check on the water level. Reserve any leftover water to use for thinning and add the cooked sweet potatoes to a blender or food processor. Puree the sweet potatoes to a consistency that your baby will enjoy.

Microwaving

Wet and wrap sweet potatoes with microwave-safe plastic wrap. (If you prefer, you can skip the plastic wrap and simply wet the sweet potatoes.) Poke holes in the sweet potatoes with a fork and microwave for 10 minutes or until done. (Try cooking in 5-minute intervals for a more evenly cooked sweet potato.) Allow potatoes to cool slightly and then slit them lengthwise and scoop out the "meat"; discard the skins. Place the "meat" into your blender or food processor and begin pureeing. Add water, formula, or breast milk as necessary to achieve a smooth, thin consistency for your baby.

Freezes well: Cooked sweet potatoes freeze very well no matter how you have cooked them or how you prepare them.

> *Quick Tip:* Baking sweet potatoes is the best method for bringing out the flavors and retaining the most nutrients.

Did You Know?

Yams and sweet potatoes are the same, and the terms are used interchangeably for the same vegetable. The word yam *originates from the African word* nyami, *which is a starchy root. True yams are tubers. They are found in Africa, in the Caribbean, and sometimes in Europe and can grow up to one hundred pounds, attaining a length of seven feet. Sweet potatoes are storage roots and seldom grow larger than two pounds each. The only difference between yams and sweet potatoes in the United States is in the labeling, the color, the texture, and the marketing. What is referred to as a "yam" in the United States is the darker reddish-skinned, orange-fleshed sweet potato. It is typically more sweet and moist. What is referred to as a "sweet potato," on the other hand, is the lighter, tan- or brownish-skinned type. This variety is more dry and starchy than the yam and is not as sweet. It tends to resemble the texture of regular white potatoes.*

Greenie Beanies

Tools: saucepan, steamer basket (optional), blender or food processor (optional), sieve or fine mesh strainer (optional)

1 pound fresh green beans

Clean and snap green beans. Add about 1 inch of water to a saucepan and insert a steamer basket.* Add the green beans to the basket and then steam until the beans are fork tender. Most fresh green beans will be fully steamed after 10 to 15 minutes.

When the green beans are cooked, drain and reserve the cooking water. (Notice how green the reserved cooking water is; it's chock-full of nutrients, so do try to use it!) Allow green beans to cool slightly, then place into your choice of appliance and begin pureeing. Add the cooking water (or plain water) as necessary to achieve a smooth, thin consistency. If you wish, you may use a sieve or a fine mesh strainer to get rid of the hulls. Let cool completely before serving.

Frozen Beans

Cook frozen green beans (purchase the "no salt added" kind) according to package directions, then puree as per instructions for steamed green beans. Let cool completely before serving.

Freezes with mixed results: May be gritty and/or watery when thawed. Beans are best when frozen whole, in individual pieces.

Did You Know?
Just 1 cup of green beans contains approximately 66 mg of calcium. If you're looking to boost vitamin K or vitamin C,

---

*You may also steam vegetables without using a steamer basket. Add a scant amount of water (about 1 to 2 inches) to a saucepan, then add green beans and steam until they are easily pierced with a fork (fork tender).

then turn to that cup of green beans and you'll get an infusion of these vitamins. Vitamin A and manganese are also found in abundance in just 1 cup of green beans.

> *Quick Tip:* Fresh green beans do not keep well if they are trimmed, cut, and then stored; they will get limp, and the texture and taste will suffer. So prepare green beans for cooking only when you are ready to actually cook them.

Sweet Baby Butternut

Tools: saucepan

1 cup baked pureed butternut squash
1 cup baked pureed sweet potatoes

Combine sweet potatoes and butternut squash in a saucepan and heat gently on low, mixing thoroughly to combine. Or you can mix the vegetables in a glass microwave-safe bowl and then heat as desired in the microwave—but remember to stir afterward for even cooling.

Allow to cool thoroughly prior to serving.

Freezes well: While butternut squash alone may thaw to a watery consistency, the addition of sweet potatoes makes thawing kinder to the texture.

Did You Know?
These two vegetables when combined will more than adequately cover baby's daily needs for vitamins such as

folate, A, and C and will also serve up a wealth of minerals such as calcium and potassium.

Quick Tip: Exploit your oven! This recipe is a great way to maximize your oven's efficiency by baking several different foods at one time. Peel, seed, and dice the vegetables as needed, then add them to a baking dish with about 1 inch of water.

Bake the squash and sweet potatoes at 400 degrees for approximately 30 minutes or until they are fork tender.

GRAINS & CEREALS

Homemade Baby Cereals—A Few Tips

Making homemade baby cereal is really not difficult. One of the best things about making baby's cereals from scratch is that you can choose the healthiest and most wholesome grains available. There will be no hidden additives like soy or dairy that may pose allergy risks for babies and cause tummy upsets. When your baby has successfully been introduced to rice, oatmeal, and barley, you can venture into other nutritious grains like wheat, kamut, quinoa, millet, and buckwheat. Don't forget, baby cereal is not necessarily the best choice for baby's first solid food. Be sure to ask your pediatrician about skipping the baby cereal and going straight to a more nutrient-dense food like avocado or butternut squash.

What type of rice do I use for homemade baby rice cereals?

It's all about brown rice. Ideally, you would want to use short-grain if you plan to cook the rice without first grinding it or long-grain if you wish to grind and then cook the rice; see page 118. Short-grain rice cooks up softer than long- or medium-grain rice. The only caveat is that short-grain rice may become sticky and pasty when pureed, so keep a watch over the rice when cooking and pureeing it. You may use a blend of any type of rice that you like; just make sure it's whole-grain. Brown jasmine rice and plain brown rice make a nice and tasty blend for baby cereals, as does a mix of basmati and plain brown rice. If you find that your baby does not like this blend, consider switching to plain brown rice until your baby's taste buds have become used to solid foods.

What type of oatmeal do I use for homemade baby oatmeal cereals?

If you will be making homemade oatmeal cereal for your baby, choose steel-cut or rolled oats. These are more nutritious than quick-cooking or instant oats, and you will not have to worry about reading the labels for added flavors or added sugars. Homemade oatmeal cereal is not only healthy and tasty, it is a wonderful comfort food that is rich in important nutrients we all need to stay healthy.

What type of barley do I use for homemade barley cereals?

Whenever possible, choose hulled barley, as it is more nutrient-dense than pearled barley. It is perfectly fine to make barley cereal from pearled barley if you are unable to find hulled barley at your local grocery store, though it is said that the process of "pearling" the barley strips out a small percentage of its natural goodness.

Grinding grains for baby cereal—storing and cooking

When making homemade cereals, you can either cook the grain without grinding it or grind the grain to make a cereal powder. To grind your grain, use a coffee grinder, a spice grinder, or even a mini–food processor: add any amount of grain you wish, then grind to a powdery texture. Store this powder in an airtight container in a cool and dry place (storing in the refrigerator is a good option).

The grains that you have transformed into a powder for cereal must be cooked prior to being served. You will find simple cooking instructions and recipes on the following cereal recipe pages. Commercial baby cereal does not have to be cooked; you simply mix it with water and serve. This is because the baby cereal on grocery store shelves is precooked and then dehydrated. It is typically made from grains that have been processed and then milled into flour. Open a box of commercial baby cereal and you will see "flakes" in the bowl, not powder or granules. The flakes occur as a result of the processing, cooking, and dehydrating.

First Brown Rice Cereal (Powder)

Tools: saucepan, whisk, blender or food processor, storage container

¼ cup ground whole-grain brown rice powder

Bring 1 to 2 cups of water to a boil in a saucepan, then add the rice powder while stirring constantly.

Simmer for 10 minutes, whisking constantly, until a smooth cereal consistency is achieved. Gradually add more water if needed. Allow to cool a bit prior to serving.

Quick Tip: Whisk! Whisk! Whisk! Whisking this recipe as it cooks will limit the amount of clumping and sticking.

Cereal has mixed results when frozen: May be a bit "rubbery" upon thawing. Add liquid such as formula or breast milk to reconstitute.

Did You Know?

Homemade baby cereals are versatile and mix well with almost every food that you will feed your baby. Homemade cereals may also be used as a thickener for purees.

❧❀❀❧

First Brown Rice Cereal (Whole Cooked Rice)

Tools: fine mesh strainer, saucepan, blender or food processor

> 1 cup whole-grain brown rice
> Breast milk, formula, or water for pureeing

Wash and rinse the rice using a fine mesh strainer. Cook the rice according to package directions (typical cooking time for whole-grain rice is between 30 and 45 minutes). When the rice is done and has cooled a bit, add it to your blender or food processor in ½-cup measurements, with the liquid of your choice and puree as needed. Keep a watch as you puree so that the rice does not turn into paste! If you wish, you may also add fruits or veggies to this tasty cereal.

Quick Tip: Watch the texture of the rice as you are pureeing—it will quickly turn into a pasty consistency if you overpuree!

Using long-grain brown rice will make a less pasty and sticky cereal.

You can add broth and vegetables to this mixture to make a tasty meal for babies between seven and eight months old.

Cereal has mixed results when frozen: May be a bit "rubbery" upon thawing. Add liquid such as formula or breast milk to reconstitute.

Did You Know?
Brown rice is more nutritious than white rice because it is not highly processed and stripped of its natural goodness.

Homemade Oatmeal Cereal

Tools: saucepan, whisk

¼ cup ground (powdery) oats

Bring ¾ to 1 cup of water to a boil in a saucepan, then add the oatmeal powder while stirring constantly. Simmer for 10 minutes, whisking constantly, until cooked. Mix in formula or breast milk and/or add fruits or vegetables if desired, and serve warm.

Freezes with mixed results: May be a bit "rubbery" upon thawing. Add formula or breast milk to reconstitute.

Did You Know?
Oats are high in fiber, calcium, protein, and even some B vitamins.

Quick Tip: Oatmeal is a versatile and nutritious grain. It makes a hearty breakfast and is a wonderful addition to foods such as muffins, cookies, and meat loaf.
    You can even use oats as a coating for chicken or fish.

Barley Baby Cereal

Tools: saucepan, whisk

¼ cup ground (powdery) barley (hulled or pearled)

Bring ¾ to 1 cup of water to a boil in a saucepan, then add the barley powder while stirring constantly. Simmer for 10 minutes, whisking constantly, until cooked. Mix in formula or breast milk and/or add fruits or vegetables if desired, and serve warm or cool.

Freezes with mixed results: May be a bit "rubbery" upon thawing. Add formula or breast milk to reconstitute.

Did You Know?
Pearled barley is simply hulled barley that has had the ends of its kernel removed. This process gives pearled barley the round shape that is so popular for cooking. Pearled barley cooks up faster than hulled barley.

Quick Tip: When your baby is moving on to finger foods, cooked pearled barley is a great way to help exercise and develop baby's pincher grasp.

TASTY COMBINATIONS

The Green Veggie Monster

Tools: bowl, fork, blender or food processor, saucepan (optional)

> ½ cup pureed green beans
> 2 tablespoons applesauce
> Meat from ½ a pitted avocado, mashed

In a bowl, mix and mash or puree all ingredients and serve slightly warmed.

Another great way to prepare this is to cook the green beans fresh, drain, and then return to the saucepan. Add the applesauce and warm through. Remove from stove and allow the mixture to cool for 10 minutes, then puree. Mash in the avocado and serve.

Not recommended for freezing: Store in the refrigerator for up to 72 hours.

Did You Know?
Green beans and applesauce are really tasty, and the addition of the avocado makes this meal smooth and creamy; you should give it a try, too!

Quick Tip: Don't shy away from mixing ingredients that you think would be horrible to taste. Babies do not "know" that green beans and applesauce should not go together.

Try not to let your taste preferences influence your baby's budding food experiences. I've suffered the presence of bananas and yogurt so that my kids might learn to like these foods.

Butternutty Apples and Oatmeal

Tools: fork, blender or food processor

½ cup cooked homemade oatmeal cereal
¼ cup cooked butternut squash puree
¼ cup applesauce

Mix and mash or puree all ingredients and serve slightly warmed. Store any leftovers for up to 48 hours in the refrigerator. This makes a yummy and nutritious meal for any time of the day.

Freezes with mixed results: The oatmeal may be a bit rubbery and/or gritty. Stir and blend vigorously as needed to reconstitute.

Did You Know?
Butternut squash and apples are two tasty foods of the fall season. How lucky that these fruits are available just as the weather is cooling and oatmeal begins to be truly appreciated for its hearty warmth once again!

Quick Tip: Consider baking the apples and butternut squash together in the same pan to save time and bring together the wonderful flavors.

Peary Bananas and Barley

Tools: fork, blender or food processor

¼ cup cooked barley
½ mashed banana
2 tablespoons pear puree/pear sauce

Mix and mash or puree all ingredients and serve warm. (You can also heat the barley and pear sauce on the stovetop and then mix in the banana to really infuse the flavors.)

Does not freeze well: Store in the refrigerator for up to 72 hours.

Did You Know?
Bananas are thought to be helpful in settling an upset tummy because of their mucous-like properties. That's right, bananas help create a slimy, mucouslike film in the stomach that coats the intestines and esophagus and protects against discomfort due to acids.

> *Quick Tip:* Don't be shy, taste this for yourself!
> You will be surprised at how tasty baby food recipes really are.

Apple Rice

Tools: vegetable peeler, sharp knife, saucepan with lid, fork, blender or food processor

    2 medium-sized apples
    ¼ cup uncooked brown rice
    Pinch of cinnamon, if desired

Peel, core, and dice the apples, then place the apples and 1 cup of water in a saucepan. Bring the water to a boil and add the rice. Return to a boil, cover the pan, and lower the heat. Simmer on low for 15 minutes or until the rice has cooked; stir occasionally during the cooking time. Allow the mixture to cool and then mash or puree as needed to suit your baby's preference.

Freezes with mixed results: May be a bit rubbery in texture upon thawing. Stir vigorously to reconstitute.

Did You Know?
The natural juices of the apples will infuse the rice, making this porridge extra tasty. Rice and apples may be constipating to babies, so be sure to serve this in moderation.

Quick Tip: Cooking the apples and rice together makes a super-tasty porridge. Double the recipe and make a breakfast the whole family will enjoy!

Six to Eight Months of Age— Mixes and More

CEREALS & GRAINS: Barley, Oat, Rice
FRUITS: Apples, Apricots, Avocado, Bananas,
    Mangoes, Nectarines, Peaches, Pears, Plums,
    Prunes, Pumpkin
VEGETABLES: Acorn/Butternut Squash, Carrots,
    Green Beans, Parsnips, Peas, Sweet Potatoes,
    Yellow Squash/Zucchini
PROTEIN: Chicken, Eggs, Turkey
DAIRY: Cheese (closer to eight months), Plain Whole-
    Milk Yogurt

Whether your baby is just starting solid foods or is a budding foodie, these recipes are sure to please. As your baby is introduced to many new foods and a few old favorites, meats and yogurt are wonderful additions to his or her expanding food repertoire and will provide extra protein, fat, and iron.

Yogurt: Plain whole-milk yogurt may be introduced to your baby at this stage. You will find that most pediatricians recommend introducing yogurt closer to eight months old. Remember that while yogurt is fine, babies should not be drinking milk until they are at least twelve months of age.

Also remember that between the ages of six and eight months, breast milk and/or formula must continue to be the most important source of nutrition for your baby. Replace these milks with solids only when your pediatrician indicates this is appropriate for your baby!

Herbs and Spices: A good time to introduce baby to the universe of aromatic seasonings is around seven to eight months of age. Fresh or dried, herbs and spices provide an excellent opportunity to add zesty flavors typically enjoyed by the whole family. Although sugar and salt are not recommended additions, there are dozens of interesting choices and the decision is yours to make. Here are just a few of the wonderful herbs and spices you can use:

- anise
- basil
- cardamom
- chives
- cilantro
- cinnamon
- coriander
- dill
- garlic powder
- ginger
- lemon zest
- mild curry powder
- mint
- nutmeg

- oregano
- paprika
- pepper
- rosemary
- sage
- tarragon
- vanilla (bean, extract, or powder)

Ideas to Spice Up Baby Food Creations

Try these herbs and spices with the foods shown to add some baby zing into those everyday foods for baby.

FRUITS	Apple(sauce): cinnamon, nutmeg, allspice, vanilla, ginger
	Pears: ginger, cardamom, cinnamon, a drip of vanilla or even mint
	Bananas: cinnamon, ginger, allspice, vanilla
	Peaches: vanilla, cinnamon, ginger
VEGETABLES	Sweet potato: nutmeg, cinnamon, cardamom, allspice, sage
	Pumpkin: cinnamon, nutmeg, ginger, dash of vanilla
	Carrots: basil, garlic, thyme, sage, cinnamon, ginger, tarragon
	Green beans: garlic powder, pepper, sage, mint
	Mashed potatoes (white): dill weed, rosemary, tarragon, garlic, pepper, paprika
	Winter squash (acorn, butternut, etc.): cinnamon, nutmeg, allspice, ginger, tarragon
	Peas: mint, garlic, sage
GRAINS	Pasta: oregano, garlic, basil, rosemary, thyme
	Oatmeal or other cereals: cinnamon, nutmeg, ginger, vanilla, cardamom
	Rice: garlic, curry powder, sage and saffron, cinnamon, nutmeg, vanilla, cardamom, ginger

continued

Ideas to Spice Up Baby Food Creations *(continued)*

GRAINS/ SEEDS	Quinoa (sweet): cinnamon, nutmeg, dash of vanilla, cardamom, ginger
	Quinoa (savory): garlic, pepper, onion, basil, oregano, pepper, tarragon, coriander
MEATS	Chicken/turkey (sweet): cinnamon, ginger, nutmeg, lemon or orange zest
	Chicken/turkey (savory): curry powder, garlic powder, tarragon, rosemary, sage, thyme, basil, pepper, oregano
	Beef: garlic, pepper, tarragon, onion powder, orange zest, cumin
	Fish: garlic, dill, pepper, tarragon, lemon, curry powder
	Eggs: pepper, garlic, onions, curry powder, cumin
DAIRY	Plain yogurt: mint, cinnamon, nutmeg, vanilla, ginger, allspice, cardamom

Did You Know?
Spices may offer additional benefits beyond zesting up a boring food. Did you know that herbalists tout the following spices for their benefits?

- *Ginger—good for tummy upsets*
- *Cinnamon—good for tummy upsets, diarrhea, possible antifungal and antibacterial*
- *Garlic—antibiotic, good for blood pressure*
- *Coriander—aids gassiness, stimulates appetite, helps rheumatism and joint pain*
- *Dill—good for hiccups, colic, digestive troubles*
- *Mint—stimulates healthy digestion, helps respiratory issues*

Stage Two Sample Meal Plan—Beginners and Intermediates

Exact portion size is not shown because not all babies will be eating the same amounts of solid foods (or even the same foods), and many babies will still be eating only one meal. Begin with smaller portions (1 to 2 tablespoons) and then slowly work your way up as baby shows signs of being ready for more.

Early Morning Waking: Breast milk and/or formula—snack if desired

Meal	Monday	Tuesday	Wednesday	Thursday	Friday	Saturday	Sunday
8:00–9:00 a.m. Breakfast	scrambled egg yolks, peachy yogurt	oatmeal, applesauce	blueberry yogurt, rice cereal	oatmeal, peaches	rice cereal, peary apples	fruits, oatmeal	scrambled egg yolks, Banana 'Cado

Midmorning: Breast milk and/or formula—snack if desired

Meal	Monday	Tuesday	Wednesday	Thursday	Friday	Saturday	Sunday
12:00–1:00 p.m. Lunch	chicken and rice with fruit dices	yogurt with vegetable-fruit mix—pears and green beans	sweet potatoes and oatmeal with pears	barley, peas and carrots, bananas and yogurt	veggie scramble, avocado dices	barley, pumpkin, peaches	yogurt with vegetable-fruit mix—try sweet potato and banana

Midafternoon: Breast milk and/or formula—snack if desired

Meal	Monday	Tuesday	Wednesday	Thursday	Friday	Saturday	Sunday
4:00–5:00 p.m. Dinner	apples, sweet potatoes	baked chicken, butternut squash risotto	creamy rice, veggie mix, fruit dices	roasted carrots, brown rice, peaches	Crock-Pot chicken and summer squash	egg yolks, yogurt, and applesauce	oatmeal, vegetable, and fruit

Before Bedtime: Breast milk and/or formula

FRUITS

Baked Apples

Tools: coring or paring tool, baking dish, tinfoil, large mixing bowl, potato masher, fork, blender or food processor (optional)

3 to 4 large apples (Macintosh, Gala, or Braeburn)
Unsalted butter (optional)
Cinnamon (optional)
Raisins and brown sugar (optional, but a must-add if you will be serving to the "big kids")

Preheat oven to 400 degrees.

Core the apples but leave the peel on. Wipe center insides of each apple with butter if desired and/or add a few drops of water. Sprinkle some cinnamon over the apples (optional). Add raisins and a dash of brown sugar to the inside of each apple if desired. Place the prepared apples upright in a baking dish. Add 2 inches of water to the dish and cover with tinfoil. Bake at 400 degrees for approximately 40 minutes or until the skin puckers and/or fruit begins to bubble.

Once the apples have finished baking, allow them to cool in the dish, then transfer them to a large mixing bowl. If you will be mashing the apples by hand, you may want to slip the apple skins off prior to mashing. If you will be pureeing them in a blender or food processor, you may leave the peel on or remove it if desired.

Baked apples may fall apart while baking—this is perfectly fine. You may turn them into applesauce or mash them gently for finger foods.

Freezes with mixed results. Both applesauce and baked apples (in chunks) freeze well, but may be watery upon thawing or have a gritty texture.

Did You Know?
Baking fruits and vegetables (also known as roasting) brings out the most flavors and also retains the most nutrients.

Quick Tips: Stir baked apples into cereal or yogurt.

These baked apples are versatile and make a great mixer for meats such as chicken or pork.

For a sweet and tasty dessert for the grown-ups, place one warm baked apple into a bowl and add a scoop of vanilla ice cream or frozen yogurt. Don't forget to sprinkle on some granola!

A Is for Apricots Done Two Ways

Tools: saucepan, sharp knife, coring or paring tool, baking dish, bowl, blender or food processor (optional)

Apricot Puree Using Dried Apricots

1 cup pear juice
1 cup apple juice or water
1 pound dried apricots

In a saucepan, bring juice and apricots to a boil and simmer for 15 minutes, then allow to cool. Reserve any leftover liquid to use for thinning the puree. Place apricots into blender or food processor and begin to puree; add the reserved liquid as necessary to achieve a smooth, thin consistency. (You may also add water if necessary.) If the puree seems a bit too runny, add cereal (if desired) to thicken it up a bit.

Apricot Puree Using Fresh Apricots

1 pound fresh apricots (approximately 10 apricots)

Baking: Halve the apricots and remove pits, place "open" side down in a baking dish filled with 1 inch of water, and bake at 400 degrees until soft and tender or puckering of the skin appears.

Steaming: Halve the fruits, remove the pits, and steam in an open saucepan of water until soft and tender. Once the apricots have cooled, slip off the skins.

Blanching: Drop whole, cleansed apricots into a saucepan of boiling water for 5 to 10 minutes; boil just until the fruits are soft. Place apricots into a bowl of cold water and slip off the skins, then cut and pit the fruit.

Puree as per directions given for dried apricots.

Freezes well: Apricot puree will not freeze solid and will feel a bit sticky or tacky to the touch.

Did You Know?
Apricots are high in beta-carotene (vitamin A), vitamin C, and lycopene. Just three apricots contain approximately 30 percent of the RDA for vitamin A. This combination of nutrients is one of the best defenses against heart disease and some cancers.

Quick Tip: Apricots may be bitter when cooked and pureed, so using half juice and half water is one way to cut the bitterness. You may use only plain water if you prefer; many babies actually like the bitter taste.

Peachy Keen

Tools: sharp knife, coring or paring tool, large saucepan, bowl, steamer basket, baking dish, blender or food processor

1 pound fresh peaches, scrubbed clean
Ginger (optional)
Vanilla (optional)

Steaming Peaches: Method 1

Carve an X into one side of the peaches and place them X side down in a saucepan with 1 inch of water. Bring water to a boil and steam until soft and tender. Remove peaches and place into a bowl; reserve any leftover water to use for thinning out the fruits. Allow peaches to cool, then peel skin from fruit and remove the pit. Place the peaches into your blender or food processor and begin pureeing. Add the reserved water or other liquid as needed to achieve a smooth, thin consistency.

Steaming Peaches: Method 2

Peel and pit the peaches, then cut into small dices. Place steamer basket into a saucepan and add just enough water to peek through the steaming holes. Steam peaches until soft and tender, approximately 15 minutes. Allow peaches to cool and reserve any leftover water to use for thinning out the fruits. Place the peaches into your blender or food processor and begin pureeing. Add the reserved water or other liquid as needed to achieve a smooth, thin consistency.

Baking Peaches

Preheat oven to 400 degrees.

Halve the peaches, pit, and place "open" side down in a baking dish filled with 1 inch of water (for a flavor boost, add a sprinkle of ginger and a drip of vanilla to the water and swirl prior to adding the peaches). Bake the peaches at 400 degrees until soft and tender and/or a puckering of the skin appears.

Once they are baked, allow the peaches to cool and peel skin from fruit (remove pits if you did not do so prior to baking). You may choose to leave the skin on your baked peaches, as it may simply melt into the fruit. Place the peaches into your blender or food processor and begin pureeing. Add water or other liquid as needed to achieve a smooth, thin consistency.

Blanching Peaches

Bring 3 to 4 cups of water to a rolling boil in a large saucepan. Add the peaches to the boiling water and boil the fruit for 3 to 5 minutes. Remove fruit to a bowl of cold water and cool for 2 minutes, then slip off the skins and take out the pits. Reserve any leftover water to use for thinning out the fruits. Place the peaches into your blender or food processor and begin pureeing. Add the reserved water or other liquid as needed to achieve a smooth, thin consistency. Add cereal (if desired) to thicken up.

Freezes well.

Did You Know?
Frozen peach slices stuffed into a baby-safe feeder are great for helping to alleviate teething pain.

Quick Tips: Once picked, a peach will not become sweeter, nor will it ripen further. A peach will become softer and juicier, however. When selecting peaches, you want to ensure there are no cuts or bruising on the fruit. Purchase peaches that are firm yet slightly yielding when gently pressed. The peach should also smell sweet and fragrant.

Peaches tend to lose their nutritional value with prolonged cooking. Baking peaches or using a microwave to steam them may be the best choice of cooking for optimal nutrient retention.

Mango Madness

Tools: sharp knife, blender or food processor, saucepan, steamer basket

1 ripe mango
Formula, breast milk, or water for thinning (optional)

Peel and dice the mango. Place mango chunks in a blender or food processor and blend until the proper consistency for your baby is achieved. Add formula, breast milk, or water to thin if needed.

Note: You may give the mango chunks a gentle steaming if you are offering them to a baby who has just begun solids.

Freezes well.

Did You Know?
Mangoes may be allergenic, though they are not commonly known to cause a life-threatening reaction. A person who has an adverse reaction will get a skin rash, like that from poison ivy or poison oak, when he or she comes into contact with either the sap from the mango tree or the skin of the fruit itself (the actual "meat" of the mango is not allergenic). Many pediatricians recommend waiting to introduce tropical fruits until baby is eight months old, so use your judgment on this one.

Quick Tips: To prepare and peel a mango, cut the fruit lengthwise, along the side of the pit.

Cut off its flesh from one side, then repeat the same process on the other side. Then cut the ends off the pit.

Cut the remaining flesh from the pit. Use a small sharp knife to peel the skin from the flesh. Dice or cube as desired.

It is easier to make your cubes/dices prior to removing the skin. Just make sure you don't cut through it. Once you have made your cube/dice "pattern," simply turn the skin inside out and slice the pieces away.

Fresh Plum Goodness

Tools: sharp knife, steamer basket, saucepan, baking dish, blender or food processor

> 1 pound ripe plums, scrubbed clean
> Formula, breast milk, or water for thinning (optional)

Slice open the plums, remove the pits, and dice the meat into small chunks. Place chunks in a blender or food processor and puree until the proper consistency for your baby is achieved. Don't worry about the skins, as they will blend nicely into the puree. Add formula, breast milk, or water to thin if needed.

Steaming plums: Drop a steamer basket into a saucepan containing 1 to 2 inches of water and add the plum chunks. Bring water to a boil and then simmer until plums are fork tender. Allow to cool and then puree as desired.

Baking plums: Halve the fruit, pit, and place "open" side down in a baking dish filled with 1 inch of water. Bake at 400 degrees until soft and tender or puckering of the skin appears. Allow the plums to cool and then puree as desired.

Freezes well.

Did You Know?
Prunes, also known to help maintain bowel regularity and alleviate constipation, are really just dried plums. Recently, you may have noticed that prunes may be scarce

*or no longer available at your local grocer. There is a move
to try to make them more appealing to a wider variety
of consumers, so they are now being marketed as "dried
plums."*

Quick Tips: Like many other stone fruits, plums are
delicate. Choose dark-colored plums without bruising, soft
spots, or cuts.

While plums will store well, you should use them within a
week of purchase. The longer they are stored, the more
bruised and softened they become.

Dried Plum/Prune Puree

Tools: saucepan, blender or food processor

1 (16-ounce) bag of dried plums/prunes

Soak dried prunes in a saucepan with a small
amount of water over low heat until they plump up, or
steam them gently. Once they are plump and tender, toss
them into blender or food processor and begin to puree.
Add soaking liquid without sparing any. Prunes tend to
take on a pasty, gluey consistency when they are pureed;
the more water you add, the easier it is to puree to a
texture your baby will tolerate.

Freezes well: Prune puree will not freeze into a solid
block and may feel sticky or tacky to the touch.

Did You Know?
The darker the color of a fruit, the higher the amount of compounds thought to fight cancer and other diseases.

Quick Tips: Always try to purchase natural prunes that have not been dried with any type of sulfur.

Many health food stores and conventional grocers carry plums that are not dried and preserved with chemicals.

VEGETABLES

Crazy Carrots

Tools: vegetable peeler, sharp knife, steamer basket, saucepan, blender or food processor

½ pound carrots (approximately 4 to 6 large carrots)

Peel carrots and then cut them into small chunks. Place the chunks into a steamer basket submerged in a saucepan with just enough water to be visible through the basket. Steam until fork tender, approximately 20 minutes. Allow carrots to cool a bit and then place into blender or food processor and begin puree. Add fresh water as necessary to achieve a smooth, thin consistency.

Freezes well.

Did You Know?
Those cute, conveniently packaged little baby carrots that are found in the grocery store are actually impostors. Baby carrots are the product of modern technology: they are cut from the Imperator variety and are specially formed by a machine that cuts them out from full-sized older carrots. Some "growers" add green food coloring at the "stem" for further effect. If you are looking for the real thing, purchase the Nantes variety.

Quick Tips: Do not reserve any leftover water to use for thinning out carrots if your baby is under eight months old, as nitrates may seep into the cooking water.

For an in-depth overview of nitrates, see page 54 in chapter four.

Roasted Carrots

Tools: vegetable peeler, sharp knife, glass casserole dish, blender or food processor

½ pound carrots (approximately 4 to 6 large carrots)
Olive oil for greasing

Preheat oven to 350 degrees.

Peel the carrots and cut them lengthwise into thick slivers. Lightly oil a glass casserole dish and add the carrots. Bake at 350 degrees for approximately 45 minutes or until carrots are fork tender and have turned dark orange. Let cool, then puree, adding water as needed to create a texture suitable for your baby.

Freezes well.

Did You Know?
Carrots are often one of baby's first foods. They are easy to digest and are packed with nutrients such as vitamin A, vitamin C, and calcium.

Quick Tips: You can cut baked carrots into little bits and serve as finger food.

Alternatively, freeze the carrot dices in a freezer bag. This will allow you to serve up some "fast food."

Parsnippity Do!

Tools: vegetable peeler, sharp knife, steamer basket, saucepan, tinfoil, blender or food processor

1 pound fresh parsnips
Olive oil (if roasting)

Wash and peel parsnips, then slice into 1-inch pieces. Place the parsnips in a steamer basket placed in a saucepan with about 1 to 2 inches of water; steam until fork tender and mushy.* Let cool slightly, then transfer parsnips to blender or food processor and begin to puree. Add water from saucepan as needed to achieve a consistency your baby will enjoy.

Quick and Easy Roasted Parsnips

Peel parsnips, then cut them in half lengthwise.
Lay the parsnips on tinfoil set on top of a baking sheet and drizzle olive oil over them. Close up the tinfoil and then bake at 400 degrees for approximately 30 minutes or until tender. Cool slightly, then place parsnips into blender or food processor and begin to puree. (Chop or mash if your baby likes that texture.) Add water as necessary to achieve a smooth, thin consistency.

Freezes well: Parsnips freeze well, but you may need to rethin them once they have thawed.

---

* Parsnips take a bit longer than carrots to steam.

Did You Know?
Select parsnips just as you would carrots. Parsnips should not be discolored or have cuts and bruises on them. There should be nothing growing or sprouting from the top of the parsnip, nor should there be little root hairs growing along the vegetable itself.

Quick Tips: Store parsnips in the refrigerator. Cut them only when you are ready to cook or otherwise use them. If you must peel and/or cut parsnips in advance, store them in a container and cover them with water; store for no longer than two days.

Yes Peas!

Tools: steamer basket, saucepan, blender or food processor

> 1 pound fresh peas or 1 (16-ounce) bag frozen peas
> Pinch of garlic powder (optional)

For Fresh Peas

Open the peapods and scrape out peas. Place the fresh peas into a steamer basket in a saucepan with just enough water to show slightly through basket. Steam until very tender; be sure to check on the water level. Allow the peas to cool a bit and reserve any leftover water to use for thinning out the peas. Place the peas into blender or food processor, add garlic powder (if desired), and begin to puree, adding the water as needed.

For Frozen Peas

Cook the peas according to the directions on the package and then proceed as indicated above.

Freezes well.

Did You Know?
One cup of peas contains more protein than 1 tablespoon of peanut butter and also provides calcium, vitamins A and C, and iron. Considering the size of a pea, its nutritional value is amazing.

Quick Tips: Try plunging hot cooked peas into a bowl of ice cold water as soon as they are cooked; this is known to help make a smoother puree.

You may also push the peas through a sieve or mesh strainer to get rid of any remaining skins.

Purely Pumpkin

Tools: sharp knife, baking dish, large bowl, potato masher, blender or food processor (optional)

1 sugar pumpkin, approximately 5 pounds*
Pinch of nutmeg and/or cinnamon
Formula, breast milk, or water for thinning (optional)

Preheat oven to 400 degrees.
Halve the pumpkin and scrape out the seeds.
Place halves facedown in a baking dish filled with

---

*Whenever you will be using pumpkins in food dishes, look for smaller, immature pumpkins. These are sometimes labeled "sugar pumpkins" or "pie pumpkins."

approximately 1 to 2 inches of water, add spices to the water, and stir. Bake at 400 degrees for approximately 40 minutes to 1 hour. The skin should be "puckery" and/or wrinkled and pumpkin should feel soft when gently pressed. Remove the pumpkin and turn it over. Let cool, then gently scoop out the meat and remove it to a large bowl to cool. (Do not scrape too close to the shell or you may find long hard fibers in your pumpkin meat.) Mash or puree as needed for your baby, adding whatever liquid you prefer to reach the proper consistency.

Note: Once cooked, pumpkin should be used and/or chilled immediately. If you will not be using the cooked pumpkin immediately, store it in either pureed form or in cooked chunks in the freezer. Puree freezes well.

Did You Know?
Pumpkins are great sources of vitamin A and beta-carotene as well as potassium, protein, and iron. Pumpkin is one of the foods that can cause your baby to turn orange!

Quick Tip: Pumpkins may be poached, boiled, steamed, or baked. A pumpkin must be cooked immediately after you have cut it open or a brownish black mold will begin to set into the flesh.

Bake a pumpkin exactly as you would bake a winter squash (acorn, butternut, etc.); after all, pumpkin is a squash!

Simmering Summer Squash

Tools: sharp knife, saucepan, steamer basket, blender or food processor

> 1 pound fresh yellow summer squash or zucchini, scrubbed
>   clean, seeded, and cut into chunks
> Pinch of basil

Place about 2 inches of water in a saucepan along with the basil. Insert the steamer basket, and add the squash. Steam until squash is fork tender, approximately 15 minutes. Allow the cooked squash to cool, then place into your blender or food processor and begin to puree. Add water as necessary to achieve a smooth, thin consistency.*

Freezes well: Squash may thaw to a superwatery consistency and you may need to thicken it up with baby cereal.

Did You Know?

The skin of summer squash is thin and delicate. Because of this, summer squash is not great for storing. Be sure to handle the squash with care to avoid bruising. If you are going to store summer squash in the refrigerator, do not wash it prior to storing. Water droplets on the squash may actually cause tiny spots of decomposition to develop. Always store summer squash in the crisper box of the refrigerator.

Quick Tips:
Consider giving patty pan squash a try. Patty pan is tender and almost sweet. It is known to some as "the spaceship squash" because it actually looks like a flying saucer. Cook patty pan just as you would zucchini or summer squash.

---

* Summer squash becomes very watery when cooked; you will probably not need to add any water for your older baby.

MEATS & PROTEINS

Preparing Meats for Homemade Baby Food—What's the Best Method?

When your baby is ready to move on to eating meats (and remember that it is not the meat itself that is necessary, it is the iron, protein, and zinc that meat contains), consider making chicken or turkey first. These two meats are easy on the taste buds and are relatively easy on the tummy as well. Meats may be introduced as early as six months of age, although the common recommendation is closer to eight months old.

If the thought of pureeing meat makes you scrunch up your nose and murmur "ick," you might consider introducing meats when baby is a bit older and able to feed himself shreds and dices of meat. Don't be surprised if he makes faces and grunts his disapproval when you introduce meat. Meat tends not to be as tasty or appealing as fruits and vegetables because of its texture.

Baking or Roasting

Baking is one of the best methods for cooking any food, including meats, as it helps the food retain most of its nutrients. Whenever possible, bake the meats that you will be using to make baby food. An added bonus of baking meat is that you can take full advantage of your oven and prepare many different foods at the same time.

Boiling, Poaching, and Stewing

When people think of boiling, poaching, or stewing meat, they often envision adding meat to a pot of plain water and then cooking it. Although you can cook meat in plain water, don't forget that using the Crock-Pot or slow cooker is a great option. You may boil or poach meats for baby food if you wish, though the drawback to this type of cooking method is that nutrients will leach into the cooking water. Many parents have found that using the broth or juices left over from the cooking process often gives the meat a strong taste that their babies dislike. This may be fine for babies who are accustomed to eating meats, but many babies who are just beginning to eat meats may refuse those first offerings. If you don't use the broth or juices that your foods have been cooked in, the nutrients will get tossed away along with the liquid. The amount of nutrients leached off may be negligible, but many parents wish to use the cooking method that will retain the most nutrients possible.

If you are going to boil or poach or stew baby's meats, add a handful of a favorite fruit and simmer them together for a tasty introduction to meats.

Crock-Pot or Slow Cooker

Using a Crock-Pot or a slow cooker to make meats for baby is a wonderful way to create a multifood combination meal. A big bonus is that the meal is perfect for the whole family, too, and you can toss any foods you want into the Crock-Pot with the meat.

Try using vegetables and spices that your baby has already had, then just spoon out 1 or 2 cups of the finished meal and puree or mash to baby's preferences.

How to handle pureed meat

Many parents report that they have great success with pureeing hot or warm meats, but the best, tried-and-true way to puree meat is to start with cold cooked meat. Chop it into chunks no bigger than 1 to 2 inches. Grind the meat in a blender, food mill, or food processor until it's almost a clumpy powder. Slowly add water, broth, natural juices, or another liquid as you are pureeing. Don't be afraid to add a fruit or vegetable into the puree. Preparing meats for babies is an individualized experiment; feel free to work with various textures and tastes until you find one that your baby likes.

You can freeze meat purees, but they will likely take on a gritty texture when they thaw. Mixing in another food like sweet potatoes or butternut squash will help smooth out the grittiness.

Can I feed my baby deli or lunch meats?

So-called deli or lunch meats usually contain high levels of sodium and preservatives such as sodium nitrite, neither of which is good for your baby. However, many grocery store delis now offer "upscale" brands of deli meat that are 100 percent natural, without preservatives or high levels of sodium. If you are going to purchase deli meat, be sure to ask the clerk to show you the label so that you can make a healthy choice.

Quick Tip: One of my favorite methods for making a tasty chicken and veggies meal is to take 3 chicken breasts (diced), a few carrots (peeled and diced), a diced onion, and some other veggies and toss the whole lot into the slow cooker. I add 4 or 5 cups of water or broth and some seasonings of my choice.

All I need to do is turn the Crock-Pot or slow cooker on low, and within 6 to 8 hours I have a nice meal for sharing with baby.

Cock-a-doodle-gobble-gobble-doo

Tools: sharp knife, saucepan, bowl, blender or food processor

> 1 boneless, skinless chicken breast or 1 turkey breast filet, uncooked and diced
> Pinch of sage

Place chicken breast, sage, and 1 cup of water in a medium-sized saucepan and bring to a slow boil. Lower heat and simmer until the poultry pieces are cooked, approximately 20 minutes. Keep an eye on the liquid level when simmering. When poultry is fully cooked, remove it to a bowl and allow to cool in the refrigerator. Be sure to reserve any remaining water. Place cooled poultry chunks in blender or food processor and puree until a powdery mix is formed. Slowly add reserved water and puree to a smooth consistency.

Freezes with mixed results: Pureed chicken may thaw to a gritty texture, so be prepared to add something to help smooth out the texture.

Did You Know?
The light meat of chicken (and turkey) such as the breast is considered higher in protein and lower in fat. The darker meat of chicken (and turkey) such as thighs and legs is

Quick Tip: When pureeing meats, add as much liquid as needed to make a consistency appropriate for your baby.

higher in iron and fat. It's a great idea to offer your baby the darker meat of either turkey or chicken: the higher fat content makes it easier to puree into a relatively smooth texture, and the higher iron is a nutritional bonus.

Crock-Pot Chicken

Tools: Crock-Pot/slow cooker

- 1 whole (6-pound) chicken, cleaned (be sure to remove the gizzards)
- Spices as desired
- ¼ cup apple juice (optional)
- 1 lemon, cut in half (optional)

Place the whole chicken in the Crock-Pot and sprinkle with spices of your choosing. If desired, add the apple juice to the Crock-Pot or place the lemon in the chicken cavity. (One or the other—but not both—is best for taste.) Turn Crock-Pot on low and cook for 6 to 8 hours (or 3 to 4 hours on high). When chicken is cooked, make a few meals: chicken and rice, chicken salad, chicken Alfredo, chicken soup…

Freezes well.

Did You Know?
Chicken is a great meat to add to anything! You could serve chicken at least seven different ways during the week. Babies often do well with chicken because of its relatively mild taste and soft texture.

> *Quick Tip:* Using a Crock-Pot makes mealtime convenient. Making chicken in the Crock-Pot will give you many meal options throughout the week—and it's a great base for a homemade stock!

❧❀❧

Easy Roasted Chicken with Apples

Tools: vegetable peeler, sharp knife, baking dish, tinfoil, blender or food processor

2 boneless, skinless chicken breasts, uncooked and diced
1 large apple, peeled, cored, and diced

Preheat oven to 375 degrees.

Place chicken, apple, and 1 cup of water in a baking dish and cover with tinfoil. Roast in the preheated oven for 15 minutes. Remove dish from oven and carefully uncover, stir contents, and return to oven for another 15 minutes; add more water if needed. When chicken is fully cooked and apple has been reduced to mush, remove from oven and allow to cool. Place cooled chicken mixture in a blender or food processor and puree until you reach a consistency suitable for your baby.

Freezes with mixed results: May thaw to a gritty and watery texture. Best when reheated in a saucepan so that ingredients may be easily recombined.

Did You Know?
The apple in this roasted chicken dish will impart a wonderful flavor and makes the meat soft, juicy, and tender.

> *Quick Tip:* Chicken pairs well with almost any fruit or vegetable. Cooking the chicken with a fruit or a vegetable offers your little one the chance to enjoy meat that is not bland and boring.
>
> Double or even triple this recipe and enjoy an effortless and tasty family entrée!
>
> Placing lemon in the cavity will give the chicken a light and airy citrus flavor.

Effortless Apples and Chicken

Tools: blender or food processor (optional)

⅓ cup chopped cooked chicken or turkey
¼ cup soft-cooked apple (no skin or seeds) or natural applesauce
Pinch of cinnamon (optional)

Place both ingredients in a food processor or blender. Add cinnamon if desired, then puree to a consistency suitable for your baby, adding water to thin if required.

Freezes with mixed results: May thaw to a gritty and watery texture. Best when reheated in a saucepan so that ingredients may be easily recombined.

Did You Know?
When cooking dinner for the whole family, you will save time by setting aside a few portions to create a baby meal.

> *Quick Tip:* Lightly mash or chop this tasty meal and serve as finger food for babies who are self-feeding.

Just the Yolks

Tools: saucepan, blender or food processor

> 3 large brown organic eggs
> Formula, breast milk, or water for thinning (optional)

Pour water into a saucepan until it is half-full. Gently place the eggs in the pan and bring the water to a hard rolling boil. Boil the eggs for approximately 25 minutes or until the shells begin to split. Remove the eggs from the pan and allow them to cool. (Cooled eggs will peel much more easily than hot or warm eggs.) Peel the eggs and separate the yolk from the white. (You can save the whites and make yourself some egg salad!) Place yolks in a blender or food processor and puree, adding formula, breast milk, or water to create a consistency suitable for your baby.

Does not freeze well: If you are going to freeze cooked eggs, do not puree them. Raw eggs should not be frozen.

Did You Know?
Pediatric authorities now say that it is fine to introduce your baby to egg yolks, even to the whole egg, as early as six months of age. If your family has a history of egg or other food allergies, please consult your personal physician about when to introduce eggs to your baby.

Quick Tip: Separating the egg yolk from the white is easiest to do when the eggs have been hard-boiled.

You can tell if an egg is completely hard-boiled simply by spinning the egg. A fully cooked egg will spin rapidly and in a circular motion. Raw eggs don't really spin, they wobble.

Scramble Me Up

Tools: frying pan, bowl, spatula, fork, blender or food processor

1 teaspoon olive oil or unsalted butter
2 egg yolks

Place the olive oil in the frying pan and warm the pan. Crack the eggs and separate the yolks from the whites. Scramble the yolks in a bowl or directly in the frying pan. Fry until the yolks are thoroughly cooked, then transfer to a bowl and mash with a fork or use a blender or food processor to puree as needed.

May be frozen: If you are going to freeze cooked eggs, do not puree them. Raw eggs should not be frozen.

Did You Know?
Scrambled egg yolks cooked with olive oil or butter make great finger foods for babies. Add cheese if desired.

Quick Tip: You may add formula, whole milk, or even breast milk to the yolks prior to scrambling them.

Veggie Scramble

Tools: frying pan, whisk

1 teaspoon unsalted butter
2 whole eggs (or just the yolks)
¼ cup vegetable puree or soft-cooked vegetable dices

Warm the frying pan with a bit of butter in it. Whisk the eggs and add to the warmed pan. Add vegetable puree and scramble until well done.

Does not freeze well.

Did You Know?
You can add the vegetables directly to the whisked eggs and scramble in the pan if desired. Scrambled eggs will hold up well with many kinds of additions.

Quick Tip: You can scramble with either vegetable puree or soft-cooked vegetables dices.

COMBINATIONS

❧❦❧

Overnight Crock-Pot Oatmeal

Tools: large bowl, knife, fork, cutting board

    1 cup steel-cut oats
    ½ cup dried cranberries, chopped finely
    ¼ cup raisins, chopped finely
    1 medium apple, peeled, cored, and finely chopped (about
        ¼ to ½ cup)*
    ½ cup whole milk or plain whole-milk yogurt

Place all ingredients in the Crock-Pot/slow cooker along with 6 cups of water, stir well, and turn cooker on to low heat. Cook overnight (8 to 9 hours). Smell the wonder in the morning and enjoy!

Mash or puree if needed and thin with any liquid you prefer. Be sure that the raisins and cranberries have reduced enough so that no choking hazards are present.

Does not freeze well.

Did You Know?
Oatmeal is a great grain to keep the bowels regular because of its high fiber content.

Quick Tip: To ensure that your oatmeal does not burn or become rubbery, turn the Crock-Pot/slow cooker on right before you go to bed. When the family wakes up, you'll have a breakfast for all to share!

---

* Using an apple slicer will enable you to chop uniform pieces.

Creamy Peachy Rice

Tools: medium-sized saucepan

- 1 cup cooked brown rice
- 1 cup plain whole-milk yogurt
- ½ cup peach puree
- Pinch of cinnamon

Combine all ingredients in the saucepan and bring to a gentle simmer. Continue to simmer on low until creamy and well blended.

Freezes with mixed results.

Did You Know?
This recipe can be used to make any quick and easy rice pudding. Use whole milk to replace the yogurt if desired and try adding raisins and figs.

> *Quick Tip:* Substitute the peaches for apricots, applesauce, pears, sweet potatoes, or even pumpkin—the possibilities are endless!

Yogurt Meals

Tools: large bowl, spoon

- 1 large (16- or 32-ounce) tub plain whole-milk yogurt
- Fruits and vegetables, pureed or mashed

Combine all ingredients, divide into portions, and freeze or store in the refrigerator.

Here are a few Yogurt Meal ideas:

Peary Creamy Oats

Blend yogurt with pear sauce and cooked oatmeal.

Creamy Sweet Potatoes and Rice

Blend yogurt with sweet potatoes and rice. Add a pinch of cinnamon if desired.

Green Beans with Yogurt and Applesauce

Blend yogurt with green beans and applesauce.

Peachy Cream Chicken

Blend yogurt with peach puree and chicken.

Creamy Tropical Oats

Blend yogurt with mango, banana puree, and oatmeal.

Creamy Tofu with Butternut Squash

Blend yogurt with silken tofu and butternut squash puree.

Freezes with mixed results: Thaw slowly in the refrigerator and stir vigorously to reconstitute.

Did You Know?
Yogurt with live cultures helps keep a healthy balance of bacteria in the intestines.

Quick Tip: You may have seen those "yogurt meals" in the grocery store, but you don't have to break the bank by purchasing them. Yogurt meals are probably one of the easiest meals to assemble for your baby.

*Live cultures help promote better digestion and maintain
the balance between good and bad yeast.*

Banana Omelet

Tools: 2 mixing bowls, whisk, large frying pan, spatula

⅓ cup whole milk
2 eggs, or 4 egg yolks
1 large banana, thinly sliced
1 cup all-purpose flour
1 tablespoon vegetable oil
1 tablespoon unsalted butter

Combine the milk, eggs, and banana in a mixing bowl.
Place the flour in a second mixing bowl, then slowly add
the wet ingredients, blending thoroughly with a whisk.
Heat the oil in the frying pan over medium heat, melt the
butter in the pan, and then add the mixture to the pan as
if you were making an omelet. Fry until the edges look
golden brown, then flip with a spatula and fry the other
side until golden brown.

Does not freeze well.

Did You Know?
*Egg dishes are a great way to
incorporate fruits, veggies,
and even meats into your
baby's diet.*

Quick Tip: Don't let the
name of this recipe fool
you—it's easy to make and
totally tasty! If you're still
put off, let's call it a frittata;
my kids won't eat a frittata,
but they will eat a banana
omelet!

Peachy Keen Sweet Potatoes

Tools: vegetable peeler, sharp knife, baking dish, tinfoil, bowl, blender or food processor

> 1 sweet potato, peeled and diced
> 2 ripe peaches, pitted and cubed
> Pinch of cinnamon or ginger

Preheat the oven to 375 degrees.

Combine sweet potato and peaches in a shallow baking dish and add just enough water to slightly cover. Sprinkle a pinch of cinnamon or ginger over the dish and stir, then cover with tinfoil. Bake for approximately 20 minutes or until peaches and sweet potatoes are fork tender (check on the water level often). Reserve any remaining water and transfer sweet potatoes and peaches to a bowl to cool. Puree or mash as needed for your baby's texture preference.

May be frozen: Some wateriness may occur upon thawing. Try adding some plain whole-milk yogurt to reconstitute.

Did You Know?

You can double, triple, or even quadruple this recipe and turn it into a delicious holiday side dish for the grown-ups and bigger kids in the family. Simply mash all the ingredients together, add ½ cup whole-milk yogurt per each doubling of the recipe,

Quick Tip: Bake a few sweet potatoes ahead of time and freeze them in chunks. That way you can take out a few chunks and use as needed in any recipe you choose. This is a great time-saver.

and then return the mix to a baking dish. Drizzle with maple syrup, sprinkle on some chopped nuts, and warm in a heated oven for 15 minutes.

❈❈❈

Summer Squash with Simmered Apples

Tools: vegetable peeler, sharp knife, saucepan, bowl, fork, blender or food processor

  2 yellow squash, washed, seeded, and chopped
  2 zucchini, washed, seeded, and chopped
  1 medium apple, peeled, cored, and diced

Place all ingredients in a saucepan along with ½ to 1 cup of water and bring to a boil. Lower heat and simmer until fork tender, approximately 15 minutes. Be sure to check on the water level and add more if needed. Remove from saucepan and allow to cool; save any remaining cooking water to thin. Mash or puree as needed.

Freezes with mixed results: May be very watery upon thawing. Stir well to reconstitute and thicken with a grain such as rice or barley if needed.

Did You Know?
The nutrients found in this mix are too numerous to name! This is a great recipe to serve with meat because the high amount of vitamin C will help with iron absorption.

Quick Tip: If your baby is able to handle the texture and does not appear to have any digestive issues, there is no need to peel the summer squash. Be sure to peel the apples if you will not be pureeing this recipe.

Cottage Peaches

Tools: sharp knife, fork, large bowl, blender or food processor (optional)

    3 ripe peaches, scrubbed clean, pitted, and diced
    1 cup cottage cheese
    Sprinkle of wheat germ

Combine all ingredients and mash or puree as needed. Serve chilled.

Does not freeze well.

Did You Know?
Cottage cheese is a wonderful finger food because of the curds. If possible, purchase large-curd cottage cheese for your little one, as bigger curds will be easier to pick up and they might just stay on a spoon, too!

> *Quick Tip:* Before you serve cottage cheese, be sure that feeding your baby dairy products is suitable. You can serve this as a meal or snack in a bowl for baby to pick at and explore. Serve as a dip for baby to dip in with finger foods like bagels, vegetable dices, and even shredded meats.

Avocado Fruit Salad

Tools: sharp knife, mixing bowl, fork

    1 ripe avocado
    ½ banana
    ¼ cup cubed mango

¼ cup diced peaches
1 to 2 drips lemon juice

Cut avocado in half and remove pit. Score with a knife so that dices or chunks can be removed. Add the banana, mango, and peaches to a mixing bowl, then add the avocado. Mix gently to combine, add lemon juice, and mix again to spread the lemon juice throughout. Mash the fruits gently, just enough to squish them up a bit, and serve.

Freezes with mixed results.

Did You Know?
If you were lost in a jungle and had only wild bananas and avocados to eat, you could survive for a long time. These are two fruits that contain 99 percent of the nutrients a human needs to survive!

Quick Tip: This "salad" is a great way to serve more chunky textures to your baby. Sprinkle on some wheat germ to help coat the fruits and make them easier to pick up.

You may want to serve this right after preparing to minimize the browning and softening of the avocado. To help slow the browning process, add 1 or 2 drips of lemon juice and stir well.

Add a dollop of yogurt if desired. Puree everything together if your baby is not yet accepting chunks and texture.

Pumpkin and Apples

Tools: medium-sized saucepan, fork, blender or food processor (optional)

    1 cup peeled and diced fresh pumpkin
    2 cups peeled, cored, and chopped apples
    Pinch of cinnamon

Place all ingredients in a medium-sized saucepan along with 1 to 2 cups of water. Heat to a gentle simmer and continue to simmer on low until the fruits are soft and fork tender (check on the water level during simmering time), approximately 20 minutes. Allow to cool, then mash or puree if needed.

Freezes with mixed results: May be watery upon thawing; stir well to reconstitute.

Did You Know?
Pumpkin and apples offer an abundance of vitamin A, vitamin C, folate, and even calcium. This combination would be great to help boost iron absorption; serve with meats whenever possible. Mix into yogurt, oatmeal, or even pureed chicken.

Quick Tip: If you let this recipe simmer for a longer length of time, you'll have a nice fruit butter!

Butternut Squash Risotto

Tools: sharp knife, large saucepan

- 4 tablespoons unsalted butter
- 2 cups arborio rice
- 2 small onions, finely diced and chopped
- 1 small butternut squash, peeled, chopped, and diced into small, relatively uniform pieces (2 to 3 cups)
- 6 cups chicken stock (use half chicken and half vegetable if desired)
- ½ cup apple juice
- Cooked chicken, shredded or diced (optional)
- 1 cup freshly grated Parmesan cheese (optional)

In a large saucepan, melt the butter on medium heat and then add the rice and onion, cooking until translucent. Lower the heat, add the squash, and cook for 5 minutes. Slowly add the stock and apple juice, stirring with each addition. Cover and simmer on low until all liquid is absorbed, approximately 20 minutes. Peek inside to check on the progress. Once the risotto has fully cooked, add shredded or diced cooked chicken or sprinkle Parmesan if desired.

Freezes well.

Did You Know?
Risotto is a hearty stick-to-the-ribs dish that can be used as a full meal with the addition of protein.

Quick Tip: This recipe will make approximately 6 adult-sized servings, so be sure to freeze any leftovers!

Tropical Butternut Squash

Tools: mixing bowl, saucepan

    1 part butternut squash, cooked
    ½ part mango, scrubbed clean, pitted, chopped, and mashed
    ½ part peaches, scrubbed clean, pitted, chopped, and mashed

Combine all ingredients and mix well, then warm in a saucepan. Mix into yogurt, oatmeal, barley, or rice if desired.

Freezes with mixed results: May be watery upon thawing; stir well to reconstitute.

Did You Know?
The flavor combination of these three foods is truly tasty. It's also packed with vitamins A and C, calcium, and folate!

> *Quick Tip:* If your baby is self-feeding, consider using diced fruit and squash and squishing gently.
>
> Mix in wheat germ or crushed cereal (for babies eight months of age and older) to boost nutrition and make the dices less slippery.

Roasted Parsnips and Pears

Tools: vegetable peeler, sharp knife, baking dish, tinfoil, fork, blender or food processor (optional)

    Olive oil for greasing
    5 parsnips, scrubbed, peeled, and cut lengthwise

3 ripe pears, washed, cut in half, and cored
Pinch of ginger, cinnamon, or nutmeg, or a mix of all three

Preheat oven to 400 degrees and lightly oil the baking dish.

Add parsnips, pears, and ginger (or another of the spices listed) to the baking dish along with 1 cup of water; arrange so that pears are "facedown." Cover the baking dish with tinfoil and roast for 20 minutes. Remove from the oven and test parsnips with a fork. Pears will likely be finished cooking. If parsnips are not fork tender, return to the oven and check them every 10 minutes. Once the dish is finished baking, remove from the oven and cool. Mash or puree as needed. Divine when mixed with yogurt!

Freezes with mixed results: May be watery upon thawing; stir well to reconstitute.

Did You Know?
Parsnips contain vitamin K and calcium but no vitamin A; that's where the pears come in. This dish serves up a well-rounded balance of vitamins and minerals.

Quick Tip: Roast everything together in the oven to get the most out of the delicious flavors of the nutty parsnips and the sweet pears.

Sweet Squashy Apples

Tools: sharp knife, coring or paring tool, 2 baking dishes, large bowl, potato masher, blender or food processor (optional)

1 to 2 tablespoons olive oil, enough to lightly coat the pan
2 medium sweet potatoes, peeled and diced
3 large apples (Macintosh, Gala, or Braeburn), peeled, cored,
    and chopped
Cinnamon and/or nutmeg (optional)
1 butternut or acorn squash, cut in half, seeds scooped out

Preheat oven to 400 degrees.

Prepare a large (9 × 13) baking dish with a light coating of olive oil. Add sweet potatoes and apples to the baking dish, then add 2 inches of water. Prepare another baking dish, large enough to hold the squash, by adding 2 to 3 inches of water and a sprinkle of cinnamon and/ or nutmeg. Place the squash "facedown" in the baking pan. Bake both dishes at 400 degrees for approximately 40 minutes or until done. Squash skin will pucker, and apples and sweet potatoes will turn a bit mushy. Once everything has fully baked, allow to cool in the baking dishes.

Remove the cooled squash and turn it over, then gently scoop out the meat and remove it to a large bowl. Transfer apples and sweet potatoes to the bowl with the squash and mix gently. Mash contents by hand or remove to a blender or food processor if you will be pureeing.

Note: Prior to blending or pureeing with the squash, remove a few portions of the apples and sweet potatoes and serve as a side dish for grown-ups. Purees will freeze well, but apples may become watery when thawed.

Freezes with mixed results.

Did You Know?
The combination of these fruits and vegetables is a veritable vitamin explosion! Not only that, but this dish

is so yummy that a few parents have forgotten they were making it for baby food. Please make sure that you don't eat all of this dish—save some for your baby's meals!

Quick Tip: This recipe allows you to "exploit your oven" by saving energy and cooking more than one food at a time. Added bonus: You'll have enough left over for your meal, too! You can save even more time and energy by baking this when you are ready to bake your main course.

If baking seems too time-consuming, you can simply steam all three foods together and then prepare as you wish.

Roasted Pumpkin with Peaches

Tools: sharp knife, baking dish, tinfoil, bowl, fork, blender or food processor (optional)

  1 sugar pumpkin, no larger than 5 pounds
  4 peaches, pitted and cut into quarters
  Cinnamon, nutmeg (optional)

Preheat oven to 400 degrees.

Cut the pumpkin in half and scoop out the seeds. Add 2 inches of water to the baking dish and set the pumpkin halves "faceup" in the middle. Place the peach quarters in the pumpkin halves and sprinkle some water over the pumpkin halves, and some spices if desired. Cover the baking dish with tinfoil and bake for 45 minutes or until the pumpkin shell turns a bit golden in color and feels soft when gently pushed in. The meat will also begin to crumple away from the shell. Allow to cool, then remove peaches to a bowl, scoop out the pumpkin flesh, and add to the bowl of peaches. Mash or puree as needed.

Freezes with mixed results.

Did You Know?
It is said that the first pumpkin pie was not at all like the pumpkin pie we know and love today. The colonists made pumpkin pie by slicing off the top of the pumpkin, scooping out the seeds, and adding milk, spices, and honey to the inside. They were then said to have roasted the whole pumpkin in the ashes of an open fire. Why not try this in your oven?

> *Quick Tip*: Save the pumpkin seeds and roast them along with the pumpkin and peaches. Toasted pumpkin seeds are nutritious and make a great snack for older kids. You can also add the toasted seeds to homemade granola, muesli, oatmeal bars, or trail mix.

Bonus Recipe: Delish Pumpkin Butter

- 3 cups pumpkin puree (you may use canned, but *not* the pumpkin pie mix)
- ¾ cup apple juice
- 2 teaspoons ground ginger
- ½ teaspoon ground cloves
- 2 teaspoons ground cinnamon
- 1 teaspoon ground nutmeg
- 1 cup maple syrup

Combine all ingredients in a large saucepan and stir well. Bring contents to a gentle boil. Reduce heat and simmer for 1 to 2 hours or until thickened. Stir frequently and check on your pumpkin butter often so that it does not burn. Believe me, it will stick to the pan and get scorched; I now set a timer whenever I need to check in on a food that is cooking!

Spread this tasty fruit butter on a raw bagel as a teething reliever for your little one, or mix it into yogurt, chicken, or anything you may think of. You can even use this as the filling for thumbprint cookies.

Creamy Salmon and Peas

Tools: baking dish, plate, mixing bowl, fork

1 (6-ounce) salmon filet
Pinch of basil
Pinch of garlic powder
½ cup cooked peas
½ cup plain whole-milk yogurt

Preheat the oven to 400 degrees.

Arrange salmon filet in a baking dish and sprinkle with water, basil, and garlic powder. Cover dish and bake for approximately 15 minutes or until filet begins to flake.

When filet is finished baking, transfer to a plate and allow the fish to cool a bit, then place it in a mixing bowl. Mash salmon and combine with the cooked peas and yogurt. Serve.

Does not freeze well.

Did You Know?

Salmon is not a high-risk fish for mercury contamination; it is an excellent source of omega-3 fatty acids and protein. Many medical resources recommend eating salmon, or another type of fish, at least once per week.

Quick Tip: Salmon is a wonderful brain food for babies and grown-ups alike. It is a perfect fish to serve to baby, as it can be moist and tender and flaky. You can cut it into flakes for finger food or mash it into other foods.

Parsnip, Apple, & Carrot Mash

Tools: vegetable peeler, sharp knife, bowl, baking dish, potato masher, blender or food processor (optional)

    4 carrots
    4 parsnips
    2 apples
    Pinch of cinnamon
    1 tablespoon olive oil plus extra for greasing

Peel and dice carrots, parsnips, and apples, then add them to a bowl with a pinch of cinnamon and 1 tablespoon of olive oil. Stir to combine. Lightly oil a baking dish, then add the contents of the bowl and bake at 400 degrees for approximately 25 minutes or until all the foods are fork tender. Allow to cool and then puree as needed, adding water to thin if required.

May be frozen: This mash may be mushy or gritty when thawed. For best results, freeze in portions that have not been pureed and then thaw and puree as needed.

Did You Know?
The colder the weather, the sweeter the parsnip will be. Parsnips are typically harvested after the first frost of the season. The cold frost turns the starch of the parsnip into sugar and gives it a sweet flavor.

> *Quick Tip:* When purchasing carrots and parsnips, be sure there are no signs of sprouting on the tops or hairs growing along the length of the vegetables.

Tropical Island Sweet Potatoes

Tools: fork, bowl, saucepan

1 cup cooked mashed sweet potato
¼ cup mashed mango
¼ cup mashed banana
¼ cup plain whole-milk yogurt

In a bowl, combine the sweet potato, mango, and banana. Add mixture to a saucepan and heat gently to infuse flavors, then remove from heat to cool. Fold in yogurt and serve.

Freezes with mixed results.

Did You Know?
This mini-meal packs a wallop of a nutritional punch, with large amounts of vitamins A and C and even calcium, folate, and iron, with added protein and fat from the yogurt.

Quick Tip: If you have leftover banana and mango, toss into a blender or food processor with ½ cup of plain whole-milk yogurt to mix in with oatmeal. Alternatively, freeze in Popsicle molds for a healthy and tasty frozen treat.

You could also freeze any leftovers in ice cube trays for use in a mesh feeder, which is a great little gadget that lets you offer larger bits of food to your baby without the risk of choking. It consists of a mesh bag attached to a handle. Foods are placed in the bag, which snaps shut and only allows small, digestible pieces to come through.

Let's Mango Tango

Tools: sharp knife, coring or paring tool, blender or food processor

½ cup cubed mango
1 banana, peeled and mashed
2 peaches, pitted and cubed

Combine all fruits in a blender or food processor. Blend or puree, adding water if needed, to a consistency suitable for your baby.

May be frozen: Some browning may occur, mostly because of the banana.

Did You Know?

Mangoes are low in fat and low in calories, but they are very high in fiber. You will also find lots of vitamins C and B in mangoes as well as iron, potassium, and protein. With the

added nutrients of bananas and peaches, this mix is a wonderful breakfast to help start the day!

> *Quick Tip:* Using frozen peaches and frozen mangoes is a great time-saver.

Chicken and Apricots with Brown Rice

Tools: sharp knife, medium-sized saucepan, blender or food processor

- ½ cup uncooked brown or jasmine rice
- 3 apricots, sliced into small dices or slivers (approximately ½ cup)
- 1 boneless, skinless chicken breast

Combine all ingredients in a medium-sized saucepan, add 2 cups of water, and bring to a boil. Cook over medium-low heat for 30 minutes or until the rice is soft, fragrant, and a bit soupy. Take out the chicken breast and cut into small pieces, return to the saucepan, and cook an additional 15 minutes. Add more water if needed and stir frequently to keep the rice from sticking to the pot. Once the mixture is fully cooked, allow to cool for 10 minutes and then transfer to a blender or food processor. Puree as needed for your baby's age and texture requirements. This makes a great finger food meal for older babies and toddlers alike.

Freezes well.

Did You Know?
Chicken and apricots with brown rice is a favorite dish of many babies and adults as well. The apricots will add

vitamin C to help the body absorb the iron in the chicken, and the rice will offer additional protein.

> *Quick Tip:* Make this recipe for the whole family!

Creamy Peachy Chicken and Rice

Tools: saucepan, cheese grater

> ½ cup shredded cooked chicken, any type desired
> ½ cup cooked brown rice
> 1 cup whole milk yogurt
> ½ cup peach puree
> Pinch of cinnamon

Using a cheese grater, grate the cooked chicken. Combine the grated chicken with the other ingredients in a medium saucepan.

Bring to a gentle simmer and continue to simmer on low until creamy and well blended.

Freezes with mixed results.

Did You Know?
Whenever you combine a high iron food (such as chicken) with a high vitamin C food (such as peaches), you enable better absorption of the iron! This mix contains iron, vitamins C and A, and lots of protein and fiber.

> *Quick Tip:* Babies tend to shy away from meats when first introduced to them. Blending meat with other foods such as yogurt and a fruit may help baby become more tolerant of the texture.

Simple Fried Rice

Tools: frying pan, wooden spoon, blender or food processor (optional)

2 tablespoons olive oil
2 eggs, or 4 egg yolks
2 cups cooked brown rice
Handful of frozen peas
Handful of frozen carrots
Shredded chicken (optional)
Pinch of garlic powder, or ¼ teaspoon minced garlic
Dash of low-sodium soy sauce (optional)

Place the olive oil in the frying pan and warm pan over medium heat. Add the eggs and scramble. Add the rice and remaining ingredients, then scramble and fry until rice turns soft and vegetables are tender. Serve warm. Drizzle a veggie puree over the rice if desired (carrot puree, butternut squash puree, and so on). Puree if needed.

Freezes well.

Did You Know?
Protein, iron, vitamin A, vitamin C, folate, zinc: The nutrient list is impressive for this simple little dish. Little self-feeders will love to pick and pinch their way through the rice.

Quick Tip: Serve this as a finger food meal. Not recommended for spoon practice, as the rice grain bits and baubs will not stay put on the spoon.

Sweet Potato Scramble

Tools: frying pan, bowl, whisk, wooden spoon, blender or
food processor (optional)

> 1 tablespoon unsalted butter or olive oil
> ½ cup sweet potato puree
> 2 egg yolks (you may use whole eggs if you wish)
> Pinch of pepper or nutmeg

Warm the butter in the frying pan. Combine sweet
potato and egg yolks in a bowl and whisk together. Add
mixture to the warmed pan and scramble with a wooden
spoon until thoroughly cooked. Puree or mash as needed
for your baby's texture preference.

Does not freeze well.

Did You Know?
*Eggs may have a bad reputation for being high in
cholesterol, but adding them to your baby's diet will not
lead to dangerously high cholesterol levels. Babies need
more fats and even some cholesterol for healthy growth
and development.*

> *Quick Tip:* Buy omega-3 organic eggs whenever
> possible. Hens fed a diet rich in flax and/or fish oils
> produce eggs that contain higher levels of omega-3.
> Buying organic eggs will ensure that your eggs are free
> of antibiotics and hormones and that the hens have been
> fed pesticide/fertilizer-free feed.

Sweet Chicken and Carrots

Tools: vegetable peeler, sharp knife, saucepan, blender or food processor (optional)

> 1 medium sweet potato, peeled and diced
> 1 carrot, peeled and diced
> ½ cup cooked diced chicken or turkey

In a saucepan, steam the potato and carrots in 1 cup of water until tender. (You may also bake the carrots and sweet potato together for a more yummy taste.) When the vegetables are fork tender, add the chicken dices to the saucepan and warm on low heat for 10 minutes. Cool the mixture a bit and then puree or mash as needed for your baby's texture preference.

Freezes well.

Did You Know?
You can tweak this recipe and turn it into a meal for the family by adding a side of rice or couscous.

Quick Tip: You may replace the fresh carrots with about 1 cup of frozen carrots to save time.

Creamy Cinnamon Applesauce

Tools: bowl, fork, blender or food processor (optional)

> 2 tablespoons applesauce (homemade or jarred)
> ½ cup plain whole-milk yogurt
> Pinch of cinnamon

Combine applesauce and yogurt in a small bowl and add a pinch of cinnamon. Stir well to ensure the cinnamon is well distributed. Serve cold or warm.

Freezes well: Some separation may occur upon thawing; stir vigorously to reconstitute.

Did You Know?
Adding yogurt to the applesauce gives baby's taste buds something to be joyful about! His digestive system will be happy, too, as the beneficial bacteria in yogurt is said to help maintain good digestion.

Quick Tip: Pop this creamy applesauce mix into ice cube trays and freeze. Use a cube or two of this frozen treat as a soothing teether in a mesh feeder. (For a description of the mesh feeder, see page 177.)

Peachy Yogurt Cheese

Tools: knife, fork, 2 large bowls, large strainer or colander, cheesecloth, plastic wrap

¼ cup very finely diced peaches
3 cups plain whole-milk yogurt

In one bowl, mix the peaches with the yogurt. In the second bowl, place your strainer or colander so that it is stable. The whey will be dripping into the bowl, so be sure there is enough clearance underneath to catch it all. Add 3 to 4 layers of cheesecloth to the strainer; be sure the cloth drapes over the edge of the strainer. Carefully add the yogurt-peach mix to the strainer. Cover the bowl with plastic wrap or a lid and refrigerate for a minimum of 8 hours. Check on the progress of the cheese every so often and empty the whey from the bowl if need be.

Yogurt cheese is ready to be served when the whey has stopped dripping. This can take anywhere from 8 to 48 hours.

Does not freeze well.

Did You Know?
Yogurt cheese can be mixed into cereals, meats, and even baby's vegetables. Try adding some to oatmeal or sweet potatoes and squash.

Quick Tip: In the event that you do not have cheesecloth, you can use paper towels or very thin cloth diapers or even a coffee filter to strain the yogurt.

Replace the peaches with blueberries or pears if desired. Another option is to use a flavored yogurt, but be sure to use one that is natural, with no additives!

STAGE THREE

Eight Months of Age and Older—Adventurous Foods for Budding Foodies

---

GRAINS & SEEDS: Amaranth, Flax, Kamut, Millet,
   Pasta, Quinoa, Sesame, Spelt, Wheat
FRUITS: Blueberries, Cherries, Citrus, Cranberries,
   Dates, Figs, Grapes, Kiwi, Melons, Papaya,
   Pineapple, Raspberries, Strawberries
VEGETABLES: Artichokes, Asparagus, Beets, Broccoli,
   Cauliflower, Corn, Cucumbers, Eggplant, Leeks,
   Mushrooms, Onions, Peppers, Spinach, Tomatoes,
   Turnip, White Potatoes
PROTEIN: Beans/Legumes, Beef, Fish, Ham (natural),
   Pork, Tofu
DAIRY: Cheddar, Cream Cheese, Cottage Cheese,
   Colby, Jack (no soft cheeses such as Brie!)

Now is the time to begin thinking about offering your baby foods that are more chunky and textured and to start introducing him to every food imaginable. This is a great time to introduce the treasure hunt in which you add bits of solid foods to other foods that have been mashed or pureed. (See page 271 for recipe ideas!) As more finger foods and utensils are introduced, adding colorful "treasures" of fruits and veggies to a plain food such as yogurt or mashed potatoes will be enticing and skill building for the pincher grasp.

The foods listed above should all be suitable for babies eight months and older, but there are still a few you should pay attention to: broccoli, cauliflower, and beans and legumes can cause gassiness, so watch for reactions; raw tomatoes, citrus fruits, and pineapple may also pose a problem because of their acidity, so you might want to wait until baby is ten months or older to serve them. If you haven't begun to do so, now is a good time to slowly start the transition to sharing all of the family meals.

FRUITS

Melon Madness

Tools: sharp knife, bowl, fork, blender or food processor (optional)

1 small ripe honeydew or cantaloupe melon

Cut melon into 4 pieces, then remove the rind and the seeds. Dice melon into cubes. Mash with a fork or puree as needed.

Freezes well in chunks: May be watery upon thawing and texture may be gritty if frozen when mashed or pureed.

Did You Know?
Melons are high in vitamins A, C, and even K! Melons do not need to be cooked, as they are typically introduced at eight months of age when baby can tolerate raw fruits. Melons may be steamed to tender and then mashed if desired.

Quick Tip: Melon may be served to baby as early as six to seven months of age, but some younger babies have been known to develop a rash from eating melon. It might be best to wait to offer melon until baby is eight months of age.

Blueberry Bonanza

Tools: saucepan, slotted spoon or fine mesh strainer, fork, blender or food processor

½ pint blueberries (fresh or frozen)

Bring ½ cup of water to a boil in a saucepan, then add blueberries and simmer for 15 minutes until soft. Use a slotted spoon or a fine mesh strainer to drain and transfer the blueberries to a blender or food processor. Reserve any leftover liquid. Puree as desired and add some of the liquid to blueberries if you need a thinner consistency.

Note: If you wish, you can skip the simmering and puree the blueberries whole and raw.

Freezes well when whole: Puree may be watery upon thawing, and texture may be somewhat thick and gelatinous.

Did You Know?
Blueberries are often referred to as a "superfood" because they contain a whole host of nutrients. Anthocyanin, the pigment that gives blueberries their color, is thought to help fight free radicals, keep collagen healthy, and promote vascular health. Blueberries are high in antioxidants and contain fiber, vitamin A, and vitamin C.

Quick Tip:
Blueberries are not a common allergen like strawberries and raspberries, as they are not in the allergenic "berry" family. Blueberries are actually related to cranberries and may be served to babies as young as six months of age.

Cranberry Jubilee

Tools: saucepan, slotted spoon or fine mesh strainer, fork, blender or food processor

1 (16-ounce) package cranberries (fresh or frozen)

Add 1 cup of water to a saucepan and bring to a boil, then add the cranberries. Return to a boil, lower heat, and simmer until the cranberries "pop," approximately 15 minutes. Continue simmering for an additional 10 minutes until skins peel away from the berries. Use a slotted spoon or fine mesh strainer to drain, and transfer the cranberries to a blender or food processor. Reserve any leftover liquid. Puree as desired, adding some of the liquid if you need a thinner consistency. (If you like, you can stir in some yogurt to make creamy cranberries jubilee, or add a drop of vanilla for extra flavor.)

Microwave Cooking

Place a handful of cranberries in a microwave-safe glass dish and cover them with water. Microwave the cranberries for approximately 10 minutes, at 5-minute intervals, until they are soft and have popped or split, then drain and puree as indicated above.

Caution! Cranberries can make a huge mess in the microwave if you do not cook them in intervals. One time I used my microwave to make a quick cranberry sauce. To my surprise, I heard what sounded like exploding popcorn and opened the microwave to find a huge maroon mess! For me, this method did not turn out to be a time-saver, as I had to clean out the microwave and then make the cranberries over again.

Freezes well in whole or in sauce form.

Did You Know?
Cranberries were once referred to as bounceberries. Because they contain small pockets of air inside them, a good cranberry will not only float, it will bounce as well!

> *Quick Tip:* Cranberries tend to be a bit on the acidic side and as such are not recommended as a "starter" food for babies. You may wish to introduce cranberries between nine and twelve months old to avoid any possible adverse reactions.

Kewl Kiwi Mash

Tools: knife, fork, blender or food processor (optional)

2 ripe kiwis

Peel kiwis and mash with a fork or puree in blender or food processor.

Does not freeze well.

Did You Know?
One medium-sized kiwi fruit, skin removed, contains approximately 23 mg of calcium and 27 micrograms (mcg) of vitamin K, not to mention a high amount of vitamin C and vitamin A. This is a great fruit to mix with meats, as it will help with iron absorption.

Quick Tip: Don't worry about the tiny little seeds in the kiwi, your baby should not have any difficulty eating them; however, you may see them at the other end!

Baked Peach Crumble

Tools: knife, baking dish to fit the peaches, and blender or food processor

    4 to 6 fresh peaches
    1 cup water
    1 cup rolled oats
    1 teaspoon cinnamon
    1 teaspoon vanilla
    ½ cup plain whole milk yogurt
    ¼ cup of flax meal

Preheat oven to 375 degrees.

Wash and clean the peaches, then slice them in half and remove pits.

Place the water in a baking dish, then add the peaches, flesh side down. Bake the peaches for approximately 20 minutes or until tender and the skin has puckered. Remove the peaches from the oven and mash in the baking dish.

In a mixing bowl, combine the oats, cinnamon, and vanilla, and set aside.

Add the yogurt and flax meal to the peaches in the baking dish and mix well. Top the peaches with the oats and return to the oven to bake until the oats are brown and toasty, 10 to 15 minutes.

Remove peaches from oven and allow to cool, then mash or puree.

Does not freeze well.

Did You Know?
For an extra boost of fiber and iron this peach crumble may be made using wheat germ instead of rolled oats.

> *Quick Tip:* Baked peaches are mushy by nature so if you would like a firmer result, decrease baking time by 10 minutes or bake until the peaches are just about fork tender.

Baked Pear Crumble

Tools: knife, baking dish to fit the pears, and blender or food processor

6 fresh Bosc pears
1 cup water
1 cup of wheat germ, toasted
½ teaspoon cinnamon
½ teaspoon ginger
1 teaspoon vanilla
½ cup plain whole milk yogurt
¼ cup of flax meal

Preheat oven to 375 degrees.
Wash and clean the pears then slice in half and remove core. Place the water in a baking dish, then add the pears, flesh side up. Bake the pears for approximately 15 minutes or until tender and the skin has puckered.

Remove the pears from the oven and mash lightly in the baking dish.

In a mixing bowl, combine the wheat germ, cinnamon, ginger, and vanilla, and set aside.

Add the yogurt and flax meal to the pears in the baking dish and mix well. Top the pears with the wheat germ mixture and return them to the oven to bake until the top is brown and toasty, 10 to 15 minutes.

Remove pears from oven and allow to cool, then mash or puree.

Does not freeze well.

Did You Know?
The best pears to use for baking an item that needs to be firm are Bosc pears. Bosc pears will hold their firmness and texture more than any other pear when baked. Bosc and Anjou both make great homemade pear sauce.

Quick Tip: As with baking peaches, baking pears makes a mushy end result. A mushy baked pear crumble can be very tasty, however, and easy for babies to manage. If you want firmer pears for your crumble, decrease baking time by 10 minutes or bake until the pears are just about fork tender.

Purely Papaya

Tools: knife, fork, blender or food processor (optional)

1 fully ripened papaya

Peel, pit, and cut the papaya into cubes. Mash with a fork or puree in blender or food processor. (If you are serving papaya to a younger baby, you may wish to steam the chunks for a bit to soften them and enable easier digestion.)

Freezes well: Papaya puree may be gritty and watery when thawed and is best frozen in chunks.

Did You Know?
Papayas contain high amounts of vitamin C (which will help the body absorb non-heme iron), vitamin A (2,516 IU per 1 cup), and even vitamin E. Papayas are also a good source of fiber and folic acid.

Quick Tip: How can something that smells so bad taste so yummy? It is not uncommon to open a papaya and think that it's rotten.

While the smell may be bad, if the papaya is not overly soft and squishy, has no dark spots or obvious bruising on the flesh, then the odds are the papaya is just, well, foul-smelling!

Pineapple Pleaser

Tools: sharp knife, fork, blender or food processor

1 fully ripened pineapple

To cut and peel a pineapple, chop off both ends, then slice the skin off lengthwise, cutting carefully to remove the "eyes." Next cut the pineapple into round slices and remove the hard core from each slice with a circular cut. Cut the remaining pineapple slices into chunks or cubes and puree them in a food processor or blender, adding water as needed to make a consistency that your baby will enjoy. (You may wish to steam pineapple chunks for a bit to soften them and make them easier for your baby to eat.)

Freezes well: Puree may be gritty and watery when thawed; pineapple is best when frozen in chunks or slices.

Did You Know?
Pineapple is a great source of calcium; just 1 cup of the cubed fruit offers up approximately 21 mg. Try mixing it into other foods—it's great with chicken, sweet potatoes, and even pork. Delicious!

Quick Tip: Pineapple is not a citrus fruit (it's in the bromeliad family, actually); however, it can be acidic.

Canned pineapple tends to be less acidic because of the processing and sugar/syrup that it's packed in, but I'm sure you'd rather not give your baby pineapple out of the can.

If your baby has shown some food intolerances and tends to develop rashes from foods, then you might want to wait to give pineapple a try till baby is around ten to twelve months old.

Poached Figs

Tools: saucepan, sharp knife, fork, blender or food processor

2 cups fresh figs
¼ cinnamon stick (optional)

Wash and clean the figs (may be stewed whole or cut in quarters). Place 3 cups of water in a deep saucepan and then add the figs and cinnamon stick. Stew figs over low heat for 30 to 40 minutes until tender, soft, and squishy. Remove from heat and allow to cool before mashing or pureeing.

Freezes well: May not freeze solid.

Did You Know?
Figs are native to the Mediterranean and Asia and are also grown in California and other warmer states. They do not store well, which is why they are often found only in dried form or when they are in season during the late summer and early fall.

Quick Tip: Preparing figs for "baby food" is a bit clumsy because of the texture of the fruit. You could mix very small bits and scrapings of figs into your older baby's cereals, yogurt, fruits, and even meats.

As a puree for a "meal," figs won't work well, but stewed figs might be enjoyed by your self-feeder.

Super Strawberry Puree

Tools: sharp knife, fork, blender or food processor (optional)

2 cups fresh strawberries

Wash strawberries and remove leaves and stems. Slice the strawberries in half or leave them whole if you will be using a blender or a food processor to prepare them. Mash or puree the strawberries and/or raspberries as needed for your baby.

Note: You can use this method to make raspberries as well; leave the raspberries whole.

Freezes well: Strawberry puree, whole strawberries, and raspberries freeze very well. Blend up an extra batch of strawberry or raspberry puree and freeze it. You can use the puree later on to make muffins or mix into yogurt or cereals.

Quick Tip: Whole frozen strawberries are great to stuff into a mesh feeder as a soothing teething reliever, and they make a great treat for your baby on a hot summer day. (For a description of the mesh feeder, see page 177.)

Did You Know?
If your baby has a history of food allergies and/or sensitivities, you may wish to postpone introducing strawberries until baby is ten to twelve months old. Considered a highly allergenic fruit, raw strawberries can cause a skin rash and, in rare cases, anaphylactic shock. Commercial baby food that contains strawberries is fine, however, because the high processing temperatures destroy or disable the protein responsible for the adverse reaction.

VEGETABLES

Asparagus

Tools: steamer basket, saucepan, blender or food processor

1 pound asparagus

Preparing the asparagus: Hold one asparagus spear with one hand at the middle of the spear and the other hand holding the stem. Bend the spear until it snaps. Toss out the lower end that snapped off. Repeat until all your asparagus is snapped.

Some people recommend peeling asparagus, but this is time-consuming, and frankly it might not be worth the trouble. The snapping method works well and takes less time. However, you may wish to experiment with both methods. Choosing not to peel asparagus will not adversely affect your baby.

Cooking the asparagus: Wash the snapped asparagus under cool water. Insert a steamer basket in a saucepan and then add water to the saucepan until it peeks through the steamer holes. Place asparagus flower side up in the steamer basket and turn the heat to medium. Steam asparagus until very tender and mushy.

Let the asparagus cool for a bit and then puree in a blender or food processor. Add water as necessary to achieve a smooth, thin consistency.

Note: You may wish to skip the pureeing step and

simply serve the asparagus by mashing it with a fork and then making it finger food.

Also note: As it does with adults, asparagus may affect the smell of your baby's urine and give it a greenish tinge.

Freezes with mixed results: Fresh asparagus freezes well in stalk form. Cooked asparagus, either in whole or pureed form, may thaw to a mushy texture.

Did You Know?
Asparagus is actually a member of the lily family. One nice thing about growing asparagus is that new spears will continue to shoot up for six to eight weeks during the growing season.

> *Quick Tip:* Mix in some cottage cheese or ricotta to make asparagus tastier.

Beautiful Beets

Tools: vegetable peeler, sharp knife, steamer basket (optional), saucepan, baking sheet, tinfoil (optional), blender or food processor

2 pounds fresh beets (approximately 8 beets)
Olive oil (if roasting)

Steaming

Wash and peel the beets (be sure to cut off the tops), then cut into small chunks. Place steamer basket into a saucepan with just enough water to be visible through

the steamer holes and then add the beet chunks.
(If you prefer, you may boil the chunks in a scant
amount of water.) Steam the beets for 15 to 20 minutes
or until fork tender; check on the water level in the
saucepan.

Allow the beets to cool and then place into your
blender or food processor and puree. Add water as
needed to achieve a smooth, thin consistency.

Roasting

Preheat the oven to 350 degrees and oil a baking sheet.

Thoroughly cleanse and peel the beets, then cut into
thin slices. Transfer slices onto the baking sheet and
brush the beets lightly with olive oil. Bake at 350 degrees
for 10 to 20 minutes or until the beets are soft and tender.
(You may wish to cover the baking sheet with a strip of
tinfoil.)

Freezes with mixed results.

Did You Know?
*When selecting beets, bigger is not better. Try to buy beets
that are on the smaller side; they will be sweeter and more
tender.*

> *Quick Tip:* Not only nutritious for your little one, beets
> are a great color to engage your little one's eyes and
> pinching fingers. Serve up some beautiful purple beets as
> a great finger food by roasting or steaming them.

Broccoli Baby

Tools: sharp knife, steamer basket (optional), saucepan, blender or food processor

1 pound fresh broccoli (approximately 3 stalks)
Grated cheese (optional)

Steaming

Chop the broccoli stems and florets into small pieces; using just the florets will often yield a smoother puree. Place steamer basket into saucepan with just enough water to be visible through the steamer holes and add the broccoli chunks. (If you prefer, you may boil the broccoli in a scant amount of water.) Steam the broccoli for 15 to 20 minutes or until fork tender; check on the water level in the saucepan. Remove from heat and leave the cover on the pan for 5 to 10 minutes to allow the broccoli to steam a bit longer.

Let the broccoli cool slightly and then use a blender or food processor to puree. Add water if needed to achieve a smooth, thin consistency.

Steam, Chop, and Sprinkle

Steam whole stalks, as above. Once whole broccoli stalks have finished steaming, chop them up and sprinkle the pieces with grated cheese—instant snack or side dish for babies who are feeding themselves!

Freezes with mixed results.

Did You Know?

Broccoli is a member of the cabbage family (no wonder it can make you gassy) and is jam-packed with vitamin A, about 19,809 IU of vitamin A per bunch (three to four stalks)! Not only is broccoli high in vitamin A, it also contains 161 mg of vitamin C and 118 mg of vitamin K. Serve broccoli with an iron-rich food and its vitamin C levels will help enhance iron absorption.

> *Quick Tip:* If your baby has had any digestive issues, it might be best to introduce broccoli into the diet later rather than sooner.

Corn

Tools: large saucepan, sharp knife, blender or food processor

5 ears fresh corn, husked

Fill a large saucepan halfway with water and bring to a boil. Add the ears of corn and boil until tender. Remove the corn and let it cool a bit, then shave or cut off the kernels from the stalk using a sharp knife. Place the kernels into the blender or food processor and begin to puree. Use a sieve if needed to get rid of the hulls from the kernels. Add water if necessary to achieve a smooth, thin consistency. (Optional: Stir in some yogurt to make a healthier creamed corn.)

Freezes with mixed results.

Did You Know?

Many pediatricians say that corn should not be introduced before baby is twelve months old because it is a potential allergen. Yet corn derivatives (such as corn flour, syrup, starch, and so on) are found in many infant formulas and commercial baby foods. It's no wonder many parents are confused and uncertain about introducing corn! Another reason to delay its introduction is the choking hazard it may represent. Introducing corn after twelve months old as a finger food may be more appropriate: an older baby/toddler should be better able to properly "chew"/mash the kernels.

Quick Tip: Compared with a majority of other vegetables, corn is substandard nutritionally; save it for when baby is around ten to twelve months of age and eating other nutritious foods, too.

Cauliflower

Tools: sharp knife, large saucepan, steamer basket, blender or food processor, fork (optional)

1 cauliflower

Wash cauliflower under cool water and peel away the green leaves to get to the flower. Chop the flower into small pieces (using just the florets will result in a softer and more tender texture). Add about 2 inches of water to the saucepan and insert the steamer basket; add the cauliflower and steam until fork tender.

Once it is cooked, allow the cauliflower to cool and then blend or puree. Add water as necessary to achieve a smooth, thin consistency. (If you prefer, you may even be able to simply mash with a fork.)

Freezes with mixed results.

Did You Know?
The flower of the cauliflower is actually called a curd. When shopping, choose cauliflower that is wrapped almost completely in its green leaves. The leaves protect the tender curd from bruising and mold.

> *Quick Tip:* Do not overcook cauliflower, as it may take on a bitter taste and be reduced to mush.

Cauliflower, Zucchini, and Apples

Tools: vegetable peeler, knife, saucepan, steamer basket, sauté pan blender or food processor, fork (optional)

- 1 small cauliflower
- 1 cup of water
- 1 tablespoon olive oil
- 1 large apple, cored and peeled
- 1 small zucchini—chopped and seeded

Wash cauliflower under cool water. Peel away the green leaves to get to the curd and chop the curd into small pieces.

Add 1 cup of water to a saucepan then insert a steamer basket and add the cauliflower. Steam cauliflower for approximately 15 minutes or until fork tender.

Warm olive oil in the sauté pan then add the zucchini and apple. Sautee zucchini and apple until fork tender.

When cauliflower has cooked, remove it from the

stovetop and add it in the sauté pan with the apples and zucchini. Sautee together for 5 more minutes. Let cool and either place into a blender or food processor and puree or simply fork mash for finger food.

Does not freeze well.

Did You Know?
Cauliflower can have a bitter taste and adding apples and zucchini help mask the bitterness. Also, cauliflower has been known to cause gassiness, so watch your baby for signs of gas.

> *Quick Tip:* Cauliflower cannot be judged by its size. When choosing the best cauliflower, look for one with a uniform creamy white color. Skip over those that show signs of mold, such as little black spots.

Eggplant

Tools: vegetable peeler, sharp knife, bowl, frying pan, blender or food processor, fork (optional)

    1 eggplant
    Pinch of garlic powder
    4 tablespoons olive oil

Peel and dice eggplant, remove the seeds, then toss in a bowl with garlic powder and 1 tablespoon of olive oil. Heat the remaining olive oil in the frying pan and then add the eggplant. Sauté over medium-low heat for 10 minutes or until fork tender. Drain any remaining olive oil (or save it to boost healthy fat intake) and transfer eggplant back to the bowl. Let cool and then blend or puree as needed. (If you prefer, you may simply mash the eggplant with a fork.)

Does not freeze well when pureed or mashed.

Did You Know?
Eggplant is a member of the nightshade family and is related to potatoes, tomatoes, and bell peppers.

> *Quick Tip:* The color of an eggplant, not its size, will tell you all you need to know about its quality. Choose an eggplant with a deep vivid purple or almost black hue.
>
> Eggplant will turn an ugly gray color when cooked.

Great Greens

Tools: saucepan, steamer basket, sharp knife, frying pan, blender or food processor

  1 bunch greens (spinach, collard, mustard, etc.)
  2 tablespoons olive oil (if sautéing)

Steaming

Thoroughly cleanse fresh greens and pick out damaged leaves. Steam in a saucepan with a steamer basket insert (water should just peek through the holes of the basket). When greens are fully steamed (leaves will shrink and appear wilted when done), drain, allow to cool, and then puree in your blender or food processor, adding fresh water until mixture is of the desired consistency.

Sautéing

Thoroughly cleanse fresh greens and pick out damaged leaves. Heat olive oil in a frying pan and add greens. Sauté until tender (leaves will shrink and appear wilted when done). Puree greens in blender or food processor, adding fresh water if needed, until mixture is of the desired consistency.

Note: Sautéing is the best way to cook greens to preserve their nutrients and gain the added nutrition of the olive oil.

Freezes with mixed results.

Did You Know?
Leafy greens, spinach in particular, are said to concentrate nitrate levels if they are not properly stored after cooking. Therefore, some conservative sources recommend waiting until a baby is around ten months old to serve homemade spinach. If you are not feeling comfortable about preparing homemade greens for your baby, ask your pediatrician.

Quick Tip: Making leafy greens part of a healthy diet is as simple as steaming or sautéing. When sautéing, add some spices and herbs such as garlic powder, basil, tarragon, or onion powder. Finely minced garlic and onions are also great additions to sautéed greens!

Just the Basics—Saucy Tomatoes

Tools: sharp knife, saucepan, blender or food processor

2 pound fresh tomatoes
1 teaspoon minced garlic
1 teaspoon dried oregano
1 teaspoon olive oil

Thoroughly cleanse, seed, and dice tomatoes and place in a saucepan with the minced garlic, oregano, and olive oil. Fill the saucepan with enough water to cover the tomatoes and bring to a gentle boil. Once tomatoes are boiling, lower the heat and simmer until tomatoes have turned into sauce (approximately 45 minutes).

Let cool and then puree.

Freezes well.

Did You Know?
Some people peel tomatoes prior to saucing them while others leave the peels on. Pureeing the sauce should break up the skins sufficiently if you've left them on, but feel free to peel the tomatoes if you prefer. Tomatoes are classified as fruits in horticulture terms, but in culinary terms, they are often referred to as vegetables.

Quick Tip: This is a plain and basic sauce but feel free to make any additions you think your baby would enjoy, such as cooked ground turkey. Add this basic sauce to just about any food you can think of!

Mash 'Em Up Potatoes

Tools: vegetable peeler, sharp knife, saucepan, fork, tinfoil (optional), blender or food processor

White or red potatoes, any amount you wish to make (5 or 6 will allow enough servings for the family)

Boiling

Peel potatoes and cut into small chunks. Place chunks into a saucepan with just enough water to slightly cover potatoes and boil until fork tender; don't forget to check on the water level. Let the potatoes cool, then mash or puree with fresh water (cooking water will be a bit starchy) or a few tablespoons of plain whole-milk yogurt as needed to achieve a smooth, thin consistency. (You may use breast milk or formula to make the puree if you wish.)

Baking

Preheat the oven to 400 degrees.

Wash the potatoes and then poke holes in them using the tines of a fork. Wrap potatoes in tinfoil if you like or bake unwrapped; place the potatoes directly on the lower rack of the oven. Bake for 30 to 45 minutes; potatoes will be done when you are able to squeeze them gently and feel that they are soft and a bit squishy. Mash or puree the potatoes with fresh water or a few tablespoons of plain whole-milk yogurt as needed to achieve a smooth, thin consistency. (You may use breast milk or formula if you wish.)

Does not freeze well when pureed or mashed.

Did You Know?
Mashed white potatoes can be used as a thickening agent for purees and are wonderful for treasure hunting (see page 271).

Quick Tip: Keep a close watch on white potatoes while you are pureeing them. They can turn into "wallpaper paste" if pureed too much.

Turnips for Two

Tools: vegetable peeler, sharp knife, saucepan, blender or food processor

1 medium-sized turnip

Wash, peel, and cube the turnip. Place cubes in a saucepan with just enough water to cover and boil until soft and fork tender. Allow the turnip to cool and then mash or puree, adding water as necessary to achieve a smooth, thin consistency.

Freezes well: May be a bit watery and/or gritty when thawed.

Did You Know?
Turnips are often covered in a thick waxy coating to help maintain and preserve them during shipment and storage. It is very important to peel turnips (and rutabagas) prior to cooking!

Quick Tip: Turnips and their sister vegetable, the rutabaga, are known to cause gassiness, so watch your baby for signs of tummy trouble.

Cool as Cucumbers

Tools: vegetable peeler, sharp knife, fork, blender or food processor

> 1 medium-sized cucumber
> ¼ to ½ cup plain whole-milk yogurt (for raita)
> 1 teaspoon fresh chopped mint (for raita)

Plain Ole Cucumbers

Wash and peel cucumber, then slice and cut out the seeds using a circular motion. Chop the cucumber and squish with a fork. Serve cold.

Baby's Cucumber Raita

Wash and peel cucumber, then slice and cut out the seeds using a circular motion. Chop the cucumber and squish with a fork. Transfer to a blender or food processor, add yogurt and mint, and whizz together until thoroughly blended. Serve as a dipping sauce or drizzle.

Does not freeze well.

Did You Know?
Cucumbers are more nutritious than many people believe. Just one small cucumber contains 114 IU of vitamin A, 5 mg of vitamin C, 22 mcg of folate, and 22 mg of calcium! However, many parents report that

Quick Tip: When you're preparing cucumbers for your little one, take the opportunity to make yourself a cucumber and tomato with mozzarella cheese salad. You could even share it with your baby!

cucumbers have made their babies and children gassy, so don't offer cucumbers to your baby until she is between eight and ten months old, and at that point keep a watch out for increased gassiness.

Sweet Potato Fries with Dippin' Sauce

Tools: vegetable peeler, sharp knife, large mixing bowl, baking sheet

 1 pound sweet potatoes (approximately 4 medium-sized sweet potatoes)
 ¼ cup olive oil
 Various spices like cinnamon, ginger, nutmeg, and cardamom

Preheat oven to 400 degrees.

Scrub sweet potatoes clean, then peel them (leave the skin on if you feel your baby can tolerate it). Cut potatoes into strips or other shapes that you may then cut down after baking. In a large bowl, place about ¼ cup of olive oil and pinches of the spices you prefer. Toss the cut-up sweet potatoes into the bowl and stir until they are saturated with the oil-spice mix. Dump sweet potatoes onto a baking sheet and drizzle the oil-spice mixture over the potatoes. Stir and swirl the potatoes on the baking sheet before placing in the oven. Bake for approximately 30 to 45 minutes or until tender.

Freezes with mixed results: Best reheated in the oven or in a toaster oven to maintain texture.

Did You Know?
Sweet potato fries are a healthier and more nutritious option than regular French fries. Liven them up for baby by offering a dipping sauce!

Quick Tip: Sweet potato fries will not cook up like regular French fries. They may be crisper on the outside and a bit squishy on the inside.

Dippin' Sauce Ideas

P'nutty Yogurt Dip (be sure to ask your pediatrician about adding peanut butter to baby's diet; remember, the "food rules" are changing!)

> ½ cup plain or vanilla whole-milk yogurt
> 1 tablespoon peanut butter or sunflower seed butter
> Maple syrup to drizzle on top

Stir and thoroughly combine all ingredients and serve as a dip for baby's finger foods.

Blueberry Yogurt Dip

> ½ cup plain or vanilla whole-milk yogurt
> ¼ cup blueberry puree or 100 percent natural blueberry preserves
> Maple syrup to drizzle on top

Stir and thoroughly combine all ingredients and serve as a dip for baby's finger foods.

Maple Hummus

> 1 15-ounce can chickpeas (garbanzo beans), drained
> ¼ cup maple syrup
> 1 cup tahini (add more or less until you get the desired consistency)

In a blender or food processor, add chickpeas, maple syrup, and tahini; blend until you get the desired consistency.

Peachy Yogurt Dip

½ cup plain or vanilla whole-milk yogurt (¼ cup)
¼ cup mashed or pureed peaches
2 tablespoons maple syrup to drizzle on top

Stir and thoroughly combine all ingredients and serve as a dip for baby's finger foods.

Appley-Yogurt Dip

½ cup plain or vanilla whole-milk yogurt
¼ cup natural applesauce
Pinch of cinnamon

Stir and thoroughly combine all ingredients and serve as a dip for baby's finger foods.

Quick Tip: Using yogurt as a base, you can mix in any type of puree or fruit sauce to make a dip for baby to enjoy. Sometimes all it takes to get baby interested in self-feeding is an ooey-gooey dip.

MEATS & PROTEINS

Lentils for Stage Three Baby Foods—Types of Lentils

Red lentils, which cook faster and smoother than other types, are best for soups and purees, and this makes them a great choice for baby food. It is thought that the red lentil will not cause gas as easily as other lentils because of its lower fiber content.

Masoor lentils are typically sold split, and they also cook up fast and mushy. It has been my experience that masoor lentils have a subtle spicy flavor that red and yellow lentils do not.

Brown lentils are those most commonly found in your local grocery store. Yes, the lentils you see are a really a khaki green in color, but they are technically called brown lentils. Like red lentils, brown lentils cook up mushy and would be a good choice for baby soups and baby food recipes.

Yellow lentils, also known as moong dal (my favorite), cook to a nice mushy texture. However, you may serve these lentils "al dente" if you add a bit of oil to the cooking water. It is said that yellow lentils (like red lentils) tend to cause less gassiness. In Ayurvedic medicine, yellow lentils are considered to be helpful for children, the elderly, and those who are ill because they are so easily digested.

Ooh La La Lentils

Tools: saucepan, knife, vegetable peeler

> 3 cups water or broth (low-sodium, all-natural chicken or
>   vegetable broth)
> ¾ cup uncooked brown lentils
> 1 large carrot, peeled and diced
> ½ cup uncooked brown rice
> 1 teaspoon fresh minced tarragon

In a large saucepan, bring the water or broth to a boil.
Add the lentils, carrot, and brown rice. Return to boil,
then turn heat to low. Simmer on low heat for 60 to
90 minutes or until the lentils have become soft, the
rice has cooked, and the carrots are fork tender. Remove
from stovetop and allow to cool. Puree if desired.

Freezes well.

Did You Know?
*With this versatile recipe, you can add anything you wish.
Try adding dices of cooked chicken, beef, or pork and herbs
or spices as desired.*

> *Quick Tip:* Lentils are incredibly easy to cook and
> incorporate into any meal. Lentils add protein and iron
> to baby's diet and also offer a texture that is great for
> beginning the transition to "table food."

Lentil, Sweet Potato, and Apple Salad

Tools: vegetable peeler, knife, 2 saucepans, steamer basket

3 medium sweet potatoes

1 large apple (Macintosh or Granny Smith work well)

2 cups water or broth (low-sodium, all-natural chicken or
vegetable broth) for the lentils

1 cup yellow lentils

1 cup of water to steam the sweet potatoes and apples

2 tablespoons olive oil

1 teaspoon cinnamon

¼ teaspoon, or a small pinch, cardamom

Peel the sweet potatoes and cut in 1-inch cubes. Peel, core, and dice the apple. Bring 2 cups of water or broth to a boil in a saucepan and add the lentils. Return to a boil, then turn heat to low. Simmer lentils on low heat for 20 to 30 minutes or until the lentils have become soft.

Add 1 cup of water to another saucepan and insert a steamer basket. Add the sweet potato cubes and diced apple to the steamer basket and steam for approximately 20 minutes, until the sweet potatoes are fork tender.

Once the lentils, sweet potatoes, and apples are cooked, remove from the stovetop and drain excess liquid from each saucepan. Allow foods to cool slightly. Once foods have cooled, combine the contents from both saucepans in a large bowl with 2 tablespoons of olive oil. Sprinkle in the spices and toss well.

Freezes well.

Did You Know?
One great way to tempt your baby into eating texture and lumps

> *Quick Tip:* Sweet potatoes, apples, and lentils are a powerful combination. This salad will serve up lots of iron, protein, and vitamin C, as well as vitamin A. Great for the whole family. Serve this salad cold or warm.

and bumps is by offering up foods that are eye-catching. This recipe is colorful as well as tasty. Add some cooked peas or green beans to make the colors pop even more!

White Bean Chicken Chili

Tools: saucepan, frying pan

- 1 16-ounce bag of dried cannellini beans
- 5 cups chicken stock
- ½ cup water
- ¼ to ½ stick of butter (either measurement works but I suggest ½ stick!)
- ½ cup chopped onions
- 3 tablespoons minced garlic (more or less to your tastes)
- 1 pound of boneless, skinless chicken breasts, diced into small pieces
- 1 tablespoon cumin
- 1 tablespoon black pepper
- 1 tablespoon oregano
- 1 tablespoon basil
- 2 tablespoons chopped cilantro (optional)
- 1 tomato, diced (optional)
- ½ jar Newman's Own medium salsa (leave out for baby, if preferred)

Soak beans in cool water for 2 hours, then drain and add to large saucepan. Add the chicken stock and the water and bring to a boil over high heat.

Sauté the onions and garlic in the butter until the onions are soft. Toss the diced chicken into the frying pan, stir quickly then add it all into the large saucepan of stock. Add the spices, and the cilantro and tomato, if using.

Turn heat down to medium/medium-low and simmer for 20 minutes. Stir and add the salsa, if using.

Simmer for another 20 minutes and stir again. Check on level of liquid and add 1 cup water or broth if needed.

Simmer for another 20 minutes and stir again. This time, add any additional spices that you feel are needed, to taste.

Last time: simmer for 15 more minutes, then remove from heat. (Total simmer: 1 hour and 15 minutes, or until beans are soft and tender.)

Allow to cool before serving and puree or mash as needed for baby.

Freezes well.

Did You Know?
This chili offers up a powerful serving of protein and iron. It will also make a nice meal for baby to practice using the spoon with, as its thickness will cling to the spoon!

Butter Baby Butter Beans—Crock-Pot Style

Tools: large Crock-Pot, knife

- 1 pound dry butter beans
- 1 pound diced uncured nitrate-free ham (if you cannot find uncured nitrate-free ham, use chicken)
- 6 cups of chicken or beef stock or water
- 1 large Vidalia onion, peeled and diced

1 tablespoon minced garlic
1 teaspoon dried basil
Pepper, to taste
Worcestershire sauce, as preferred (optional)

Wash the beans and pick out any debris. Place all ingredients in a Crock-Pot and cook on high for 6 hours. Turn Crock-Pot to low and cook for another 2 hours.

Check on liquid level and add more if you desire a thinner consistency.

Freezes well.

Did You Know?
This basic recipe for butter beans may be souped up with the addition of vegetables such as diced carrots, tomatoes, parsnips, peppers, or even mushrooms. You can also add a cup of uncooked rice to make it more hearty.

Legumes for Stage Three Baby Foods—Types of Legumes

Legumes are very nutritious as they are full of protein, iron, calcium, and fiber. There are a variety of ways to incorporate legumes into your baby's diet. You can prepare and then puree or mash legumes or simply offer them up a finger food. Adding legumes to a stew or soup base is a tasty way to cook them for baby.

There are many different varieties of legumes, a class of vegetable that includes beans, peas, and lentils. Each kind can have several different names and the names can vary depending on what part of the world you hail from. Your red bean could be my kidney bean and your lima bean may be my butter bean. Lentils are also legumes although many of us do not think of the lentil when we think of legumes. Here are a few common types of legumes:

Pinto Beans There is no mistaking this bean for another. Pinto beans are light tan with an almost purple mottled shell. The name pinto bean literally means "painted bean." Pinto beans can be cooked to a very creamy texture, and they are probably best known as the beans that are used in Mexican refried beans.

Black-Eyed Peas Perhaps the most recognizable of legumes, the black-eyed pea is a tiny little thing with a black "eye" at its center curve. Also known as "cow peas," these legumes are great in soups, stews, in rice dishes, and even in cold salads.

Butter Beans These rather large beans are a creamy yellow color. They are sometimes called lima beans but the butter bean and the lima bean are technically not the same. Butter beans are actually Fordhook beans. The little green beans that many of us know as lima beans are a different variety. I personally find the taste of butter beans far superior to the taste of lima beans. Butter beans are very nutritious and contain lots of fiber, iron, and protein, too. They make great finger food for babies who do well with self-feeding. When cooked they can be a bit slippery and elusive, and your baby may have difficulty chasing them around the plate.

Red Beans Red beans are best described as kidney beans. For some, small kidney beans are known as red beans though others may refer to the small field pea or adzuki bean as the red bean. All confusion aside, whatever version of the red bean you choose to prepare will pack a nutritional punch. The color of the beans will catch your little one's eye and stir some interest.

Lovely Legumes

Tools: large saucepan, mesh strainer, blender or food processor

1 cup dried legumes

Rinse and pick through the beans to remove any debris. Add 3 cups of water to a large saucepan along with the legumes. Bring contents to a boil and then lower the heat to a simmer; be sure to cover the pot and add more water as needed. Cook longer for a mushier legume and more quickly for a firmer legume; the texture choice is yours. Once the legumes are cooked, puree if needed, using fresh water.

Freezes well.

Did You Know?
The method of cooking legumes does not change no matter what type you are preparing. Soaking beans overnight is not necessary and will not affect the end result; soaking simply reduces the length of the cooking time.

Quick Tip: Beans and other legumes should typically be introduced when baby is between eight and ten months old.

Simple, Fantastic Fish

Tools: frying pan

1 (1-pound) haddock or cod filet
Spices if desired (garlic, onion, tarragon, dill, for example)

Pat filet dry with a paper towel. In a frying pan large enough to lay the fish flat, place spices and enough water to slightly cover the filet. Add the fish and poach (a fancy way of saying simmer) until it turns totally white. Remove from heat and let the fish sit for 5 minutes to complete cooking. Chop, crumble, mash, or puree the poached fish and serve.

Freezes well whole.

Did You Know?
Fish is one of the few sources of complete protein, and this alone should place fish on your plate at least once a week! The omega-3s in fish are powerful indeed and may even help little ones who have eczema or other skin ailments.

Quick Tip: While fish filets may be deboned, it is a good idea to pick through the filet prior to cooking and serving to make sure that bones were not overlooked!

Consider poaching this fish in a tasty homemade stock or other type of broth instead of water. Delicious!

Chicken in a Packet

Tools: vegetable peeler, sharp knife, tinfoil, cookie sheet

    4 boneless, skinless chicken breast halves
    2 tablespoons olive oil to drizzle
    Paprika, garlic powder, basil, oregano
    2 medium peeled carrots, cut in small strips
    1 cup mushroom slices
    ½ small onion, chopped

2 medium zucchinis, sliced (peel the zucchini for older babies if desired)

Preheat oven to 400 degrees.

Roll off 4 large pieces of tinfoil and place 1 chicken breast half on each sheet. Drizzle 1 tablespoon of olive oil over the chicken breasts, then sprinkle with the spices. Add veggies to each chicken breast and drizzle with the rest of the oil. Close the tinfoil to make packets. Arrange the tinfoil packets on a cookie sheet, then place inside the oven and bake for 30 to 35 minutes. (You can also toss the packets on the grill. If grilling, keep the tinfoil on a rack where the temperature is medium-high and grill for 25 minutes.)

Freezes with mixed results.

Did You Know?
Making meals in a packet is not only simple and fast, it's highly nutritious, as the food and all its nutrients are cooked and infused together.

Quick Tip: Part of the fun of packets is serving the food directly from the oven to the table. If you wish to do this, make sure the packet and food are cool enough so that no one burns their fingers!

Crock-Pot/Slow Cooker Pork Tenderloin

Tools: Crock-Pot or slow cooker, small bowl, sharp knife, fork

1 pork tenderloin (about 2 pounds)
1 cup water or low-sodium natural chicken broth
½ cup apple juice
Shake of pepper
Shake of nutmeg

1 small onion, finely diced
1 tablespoon minced garlic

Place tenderloin in the Crock-Pot. In a small bowl, mix water and juice, add the pepper and nutmeg, and stir. Pour half of the liquid over the tenderloin, then turn over and add the rest of the liquid. Add the onions and garlic and stir it up. Turn the Crock-Pot on low and cook for approximately 6 hours or until the tenderloin begins to fall apart.

When pork is done, remove to a cutting surface and shred with a knife and fork, much as you would do when "pulling pork." Make sure the size of the pieces you offer your baby won't pose a choking hazard.

Freezes with mixed results.

Did You Know?
Pork tenderloin is one of the leanest and most tender cuts of pork available. This makes it an ideal choice for the baby who is just exploring meats served in shreds or pieces.

Quick Tip: Using a slow cooker will make most meats soft, tender, and easy to shred into bits and pieces. You can toss the meat into the Crock-Pot and add any liquids and herbs and spices you desire; add veggies, lentils, and other legumes, too!

Beef It Up!

Tools: sharp knife, blender or food processor

1 cup uncooked round roast or top sirloin beef

Roast the beef in the oven on a rack, over a shallow

baking dish, at 375 degrees until the juices run clear, and the internal temperature is 160 degrees. Approximate cooking time: 20 minutes per pound. Let cool, then slice into chunks no bigger than 1 inch each.

Place beef chunks in blender or food processor and puree until a powdery mix is formed. Slowly add ¼ cup water and puree further until a smooth consistency is created. You may add veggies or fruits to this puree as you like.

Optional: Shred the meat using a cheese grater and serve as finger food; mix in veggies or fruit as you like.

Freezes with mixed results: May be gritty when thawed.

Did You Know?
Beef is an amazing source of protein, with 29.73 grams of protein per 100 grams of meat—wow!

Quick Tip: Eye of round roast, top sirloin, and lean fresh ground beef are just three cuts of beef that are good to use for baby food.

Oatmeal Cod

Tools: 3 bowls, large frying pan or baking sheet, spatula, paper towels

Garlic powder, paprika, basil, and pepper to your taste
2 tablespoons all-purpose flour
½ cup olive oil and ½ cup vegetable oil for frying (more or less depending on the size of your pan)
1 egg
⅓ cup whole milk
2 cups regular oats
4 to 5 small cod or haddock filets—1½ to 2 pounds of fish

Frying

In a bowl, add spices and herbs to the flour and mix. Warm the oil in a large frying pan over medium-high heat. In another bowl, whisk the egg and milk until a bit frothy. Put the oats in a third bowl. Dip and coat the fish filets in the flour (be sure to shake off any excess flour). Next, dip the fish into the egg mixture, then dip it into the oats and thoroughly coat. Fry the fish in the heated oil for approximately 3 minutes on one side, then turn over and fry about 3 minutes on the other side. Depending on the size and thickness of the fish, you might need to fry for a longer/shorter length of time. Once the filets are fried, drain on paper towels and allow to cool before serving.

Baking

Preheat the oven to 350 degrees and coat a baking sheet with olive oil.

Season and coat the fish as directed above and keep the coated filets on a plate. Once the oven temperature has reached 350 degrees put the baking sheet in the oven to warm up. Wait 5 minutes, then add the fish to the sheet. Bake for 5 to 10 minutes depending on thickness of fish, then flip and bake until flaking (approximately 10 more minutes).

Freezes well: Best reheated in a toaster oven or oven.

Did You Know?
Baking fish is not only more healthy, it preserves more of the

Quick Tip: Serve with a dipping sauce for baby—mix yogurt, dill, and a bit of lemon juice.

nutrients in the fish, results in a better texture, and brings out the more delicate flavors.

Totally Tofu

Tools: paper towels, sharp knife

1 block firm tofu (about 16 ounces)

Open the package of tofu, drain the water, then rinse with fresh cold water and blot the tofu dry with paper towels. Slice it according to use. If you'll be blending or mashing it, it is a good idea to slice it into small cubes. Blend it with other foods, sauté it, or serve raw in chunks.

Freezes with mixed results: Tofu does freeze, but it will turn more spongy in texture and often changes to a darkish caramel color.

Did You Know?
One of the best things about tofu is that it takes on any flavor you choose. Tofu has many uses and is great as a finger food for baby, an addition to soups, or a substitute for meats.

> *Quick Tip:* Tofu is often overlooked as a baby food, and it is sometimes "feared" by many. Tofu has a strange sort of mystique about it; it's seen as an odd, spongy-looking glob, and many people have no idea what to do with it.
>
> With so many conflicting studies about the goodness or potential dangers of soy, this food option is a personal choice.

Really Perfect Pork

Tools: Crock-Pot/slow cooker or large shallow saucepan, blender or food processor (optional)

    1 to 2 pounds pork tenderloin
    water to cover
    1 to 3 cups apple juice or water
    Pinch of cinnamon or ginger

In a Crock-Pot or slow cooker (or large shallow saucepan), place the tenderloin and just enough water to cover. Mix the juice and cinnamon (or ginger), stir, then pour half of the liquid over the tenderloin. Turn over the tenderloin and add the rest of the liquid.

Turn the Crock-Pot on low and cook for approximately 6 hours (if using a saucepan, turn heat on, cover, and simmer for 3 to 4 hours). Be sure to check on the water levels and add more if needed. Once the meat is fully cooked, allow to cool and then cut into chunks if you will be pureeing. If you are not going to puree, shred and chop the meat into bite-sized pieces.

Freezes well.

Did You Know?
Pork is a good source of vitamin D, has about 5 mg of calcium per 100 grams, and also contains niacin (B_3) and thiamin (B_1). Pork is also versatile. Sauté it for a noodle or rice dish, roast it for a traditional dinner, or even use it to make meatballs.

Quick Tip: Cooking pork with a liquid such as apple juice or water with a hint of cinnamon is a wonderful option for great flavor and texture.

GRAINS & SEEDS

Tips for Preparing Grains and Seeds

For many of the grain recipes found on the next pages, toasting and/or rinsing the grains may help to impart a sweeter and more satisfying flavor. While these steps are not necessary, many cooks like to do this to lessen the slight bitterness in some grains; others are simply tastier when pre-prepared. (One big advantage of toasting grains is that they take less time to cook this way.)

To rinse grains, use a fine mesh strainer placed in your sink. Add the amount of grains desired and then rinse until the water runs clear and/or bubbles are no longer rising from the grains.

To toast, simply warm a large frying pan over medium-high heat and then add the grains. Stir continuously until the grains turn a darker color and you can smell an almost nutty aroma. You can also toast grains in your oven: preheat the oven to 350 degrees, then spread out a thin layer of grains on a baking sheet. Place the baking sheet in the oven and toast for ten to fifteen minutes. The grains will turn dark and the aroma will be slightly nutty.

Here are a few grains that you might want to consider toasting and/or rinsing prior to cooking.

Quinoa

Quinoa (which is actually a seed, not a grain) contains a natural coating of saponins that may give it a bitter taste. As a result, quinoa is usually rinsed and washed prior to packaging, but some of the saponins may still be found as a slight powder coating the surface.

To rinse, simply add the desired amount to a fine mesh strainer and run cool water over it. Quinoa will be considered fully rinsed when there are no longer bubbles appearing and the water runs clear. You can toast quinoa in a frying pan or in the oven.

Millet

Millet really benefits from toasting, either on the stovetop or in the oven.

Barley

Barley is wonderful for toasting, as it brings out a very rich, nutty flavor that is nice for soups and stir-fry.

Oats

Oats do not have to be toasted, but you may want to try it for a sweet nutty flavor.

Kamut

Kamut does not need to be toasted, but when it is, it brings a crunchy texture to the dish you are preparing. Toasted kamut is great in cookies, veggie burgers, and pilafs. Many people purchase stone-milled or stone-ground kamut for use in cereals; this type does not need to be washed or rinsed.

Buckwheat/Kasha

Like quinoa, buckwheat is also a seed and not a grain. It is not related to wheat. Buckwheat should be rinsed prior to preparing. Kasha is simply buckwheat seed that has already been roasted. If you want to make your own kasha, all you need to do is roast buckwheat!

Quinoa

Tools: saucepan

1 cup quinoa

In a saucepan, bring 2 cups of water to a boil and then add the quinoa. Stir, cover, and turn heat to low; simmer for 15 minutes. Allow to cool and serve with fruits, veggies, yogurt, or whatever you like.

Note: Quinoa may be ground in a coffee grinder if you wish to make a fine, thin cereal (see reference on page 117.)

Freezes with mixed results.

Did You Know?
Quinoa is considered a complete protein. Just 1 cup contains approximately 22 grams of protein. It has been grown in South America for thousands of years. The Incas considered quinoa the "mother grain"—a true life sustainer!

Quick Tip: If you have never cooked quinoa before, you may be a bit frightened off by the cooked result. My kids call quinoa the alien grain because when it cooks, it "pops" into spirals and disks.

Creamy Sunshine Quinoa

Tools: saucepan

1 cup quinoa, rinsed
½ cup papaya puree

¼ cup strawberry puree
2 tablespoons plain whole-milk yogurt, more if desired

In a saucepan, bring 2 cups of water to a boil and then add the quinoa. Stir, then cover and turn heat to low; simmer for 15 minutes. When the quinoa is fully cooked, fold in the papaya and strawberry puree and return to heat to infuse ingredients. Serve warm as a breakfast cereal, mixing in the yogurt.

Makes approximately 3 cups.

Freezes with mixed results.

Did You Know?
Quinoa is good for breakfast, snack, or dinnertime! Use your imagination.

Quick Tip: Quinoa may be made soupier by adding an extra ½ cup of water.

Kamut

Tools: saucepan, blender or food processor (optional)

1 cup kamut, stone-ground "flakes"

In a saucepan, bring 3 cups of water to a boil and then add the kamut. Stir, cover, and turn heat to low; simmer for 15 minutes. Allow to cool and serve with fruits, veggies, yogurt, or whatever you like. Puree if needed.

Makes approximately 3 cups.

Freezes with mixed results.

Did You Know?
Kamut is loosely related to wheat, but it is said that people with a wheat protein allergy are able to eat it without issues. However, kamut is not for those with celiac disease, even though the level of gluten may not be as high as in wheat.

Quick Tip: If you have whole kamut grains, often called berries, you may grind them to a powder in a coffee grinder or food processor for a thin cereal.

Call Me Buckwheat—Call Me Kasha

Tools: saucepan

½ cup roasted buckwheat/kasha

In a saucepan, bring 2 cups of water to a boil and then add the kasha. Stir, cover, and turn heat to low; simmer for 10 to 15 minutes. Allow to cool and serve with fruits, veggies, yogurt, or whatever you like.

Makes approximately 2 cups.

Freezes with mixed results.

Did You Know?
As mentioned on page 231, buckwheat is actually a seed and is not related to wheat. Very nutritious, buckwheat flour makes a hearty, dense pancake, muffin, and cookie, while kasha is wonderful in pilaf, soups, and even meatballs and meat loaf.

Quick Tip: Cooking buckwheat is as simple as cooking rice. You can prepare it in a variety of ways and add it to almost any food you like!

Millet (Dry and Fluffy)

Tools: saucepan, fork

½ cup millet (rinsed, then toasted)

In a saucepan, bring 1 cup of water to a boil and then add the millet. Stir well, cover, and turn heat to low; simmer for 20 to 25 minutes until the water is absorbed. Fluff with a fork and allow to cool. Serve mixed with fruits, veggies, meats, or whatever you like.

> *Quick Tip:* If you soak whole-grain millet for a few hours, you may cook it like rice; it will take about 20 minutes. Millet will add texture to soups and stews. For cooking the whole grain, a good rule of thumb is 1 cup of millet per 2 to 3 cups of water.

Millet (Wet and Soupy)

½ cup millet (rinsed, then toasted)

In a saucepan, bring 1½ cups of water to a boil and then add the millet. Stir well, cover, and turn heat to low; simmer for 20 to 25 minutes until the water is absorbed. Fluff with a fork and allow to cool a bit. This method yields a result that is better for cereal. Mix with fruits, veggies, or whatever you like.

Freezes with mixed results.

Did You Know?
Millet is rich in B vitamins, potassium, phosphorus, magnesium, and iron and is even considered a good protein source.

IT'S A FREE-FOR-ALL WITH DELICIOUS COMBINATIONS AND MORE!

Table Foods, Family Meals, and Tasty Wholesome Snacks!

This section of stage three for babies eight months and older is where you'll find amazing ideas and recipes that the whole family can share. Until your baby begins to eat a larger variety of foods with more textures, you might feel like a short-order cook. Now is the time to use all those foods and simple recipes to create new and more appealing, tastier meals. As the emphasis shifts to finger foods and self-feeding, making quick meals or finger food snacks becomes easy.

Simple Ideas and Ways to Use Fruits, Vegetables, and Other Foods as Finger Foods

Fruits

Colorful and highly nutritious, small soft bits of fruit will have your baby's fingers pinching away for hours. Be sure to take out any seeds or pits before serving, though. One easy way to make finger foods from fruits is to use a cheese grater and grate fruits like apples, pears, and even melons. Use wheat germ or crush up Cheerios or other cold cereals to make a "dust" and coat slippery fruits for easier pickup. You can even shake on some spices to liven up the fruits!

- soft baked peaches, diced
- small dices of ripe banana

- small bits of ripe mango
- dices of ripe pears
- small dices of melon
- small bits of avocado
- squished blueberries
- small dices of kiwi (seeds should be okay for baby over ten months old)
- small dices of mixed fruits for a finger fruit salad

Vegetables

Be sure veggies are soft-cooked, seeded, and peeled as needed. Try roasting or steaming some veggies for yummy finger foods! Don't forget the herbs and spices for extra taste appeal.

- dices of soft-baked sweet potato or sweet potato fries
- dices of soft-baked white potato
- small dices of soft-cooked carrots
- small dices of soft-cooked peas
- small dices of soft-cooked broccoli
- small bits of soft-cooked green beans
- small bits of soft-baked butternut or acorn squash
- small dices of soft-cooked veggies mixed as a "veggie salad"

Other Foods

Finger foods can be more than simple fruits and vegetables. Try some of these ideas:

- tofu diced into tiny cubes and coated with cereal dust or wheat germ
- soft-cooked pasta (ditalini or cut-up rotini, rigatoni, fusilli, or shells)
- small bits of pasteurized soft cheeses like cheddar, Jack, Gouda, and so on.

- small dices or shreds of soft-cooked chicken, fish, beef, or turkey (mix with baby's favorite puree as a sauce)
- cereals such as multigrain Cheerios or Oatie-Os
- petite toast points with a fruit puree or a thin layer of cream cheese
- scrambled whole eggs or egg yolks

Sweet Potato, Apples, & Chicken in a Pot

Tools: vegetable peeler, sharp knife, large saucepan, bowl, potato masher (optional), blender or food processor (optional)

1 boneless, skinless chicken breast, uncooked and diced
1 or 2 medium-sized apples (Macintosh are best) peeled, cored, and diced
½ cup peeled and diced sweet potato
2 cups water or chicken or vegetable stock

Combine all ingredients in a large saucepan. Bring to a slow boil and then lower the heat to simmer until the chicken pieces are cooked, approximately 20 minutes. Keep an eye on the liquid level when simmering.

When the chicken is fully cooked and the apples and sweet potato are mushy, remove contents to a bowl and allow to cool. Puree, mash, or chop to a consistency suitable for your baby, adding the leftover cooking liquid to thin if required.

Quick Tip: Double this recipe and turn it into a hearty "stew" for the whole family. Simply add 1 or 2 cups of cooked rice after cooking and mix.

Freezes well: A bit of separation may occur upon thawing, and meat may turn a bit gritty.

Did You Know?
A yummy way to make chicken is to boil diced or chopped pieces in a scant amount of water with added veggies and a dash of herbs or spices such as basil or garlic powder.

Groovy Grape Chicken with Noodles

Tools: blender or food processor

- 1 boneless, skinless chicken breast, cooked (see page 149 for cooking methods)
- ½ cup grapes
- Splash of pear juice
- Pinch of sage and ginger
- 1 cup cooked noodles, chopped into manageable pieces

Combine chicken, grapes, juice, and spices in a blender or food processor and chop or puree to a consistency that your baby will enjoy. Warm chicken and grapes in a saucepan, then serve mixed into noodles.

Makes approximately 2 servings.

Freezes with mixed results.

Did You Know?
The combination of chicken and grapes contains vitamin A, vitamin C, folate, calcium, protein, and niacin. Who

Quick Tip: If you have the time, cut grapes into quarters and mix with shredded chicken instead of chopping or pureeing. This will make a nice finger food meal!

knew that this mix would taste so good while providing so many nutrients?

✿

Cheesy Pasta with Asparagus

Tools: steamer basket, 2 saucepans

    1 pound asparagus
    ½ box (8 ounces) ditalini or any shape pasta you prefer
    1 cup shredded cheddar cheese

Trim and steam asparagus in a steamer basket in one saucepan. In another saucepan, cook pasta according to package directions. When pasta and asparagus are finished cooking, drain and transfer both to one saucepan (use only the soft asparagus tops). Blend in cheddar cheese and allow to melt, or make a cheese sauce (below) and toss pasta and asparagus with the sauce.

Freezes with mixed results.

Did You Know?
This dish is full of protein, vitamin C, iron, and calcium.

Quick Tip: Substitute ricotta for cheddar for a creamy and lighter flavor.

✿

Cheesy Sauce for Vegetables, Pasta, and Meats

Tools: saucepan, whisk

2 tablespoons unsalted butter
2 tablespoons all-purpose flour
1 to 1½ cups whole milk
½ to 1 cup shredded cheese (cheddar, Jack, and Colby
    together are very good, but use any type of cheese you
    prefer)

In a saucepan, melt butter and stir in flour to make
a thin paste. Cook 1 to 2 minutes, stirring constantly.
Whisk in milk a little at a time to make a white sauce.
Bring to a boil, then reduce heat and simmer while
whisking. Remove saucepan from heat and stir in cheese,
or keep the saucepan on low heat and stir constantly until
the cheese is melted.

Does not freeze well.

Did You Know?
*A true roux is made by using
equal weights of a fat and
flour. If you are using ½ cup
of butter, then you would
use 1 cup of flour, as each of
these weigh approximately
4 ounces. Using the literal
1:1 ratio works just as well.*

Quick Tip: The base for
many cheese sauces and
gravies is called a "roux."
Use equal parts butter
and flour, then add milk
as needed to achieve the
saucy texture you desire.
Add cheese as needed to
give the cheese sauce your
desired thickness.

Sweet Lentil Chicken Stew

Tools: vegetable peeler, sharp knife, large saucepan, fork,
blender or food processor (optional)

¾ cup red lentils

1 small sweet potato, peeled and diced

1 uncooked boneless, skinless chicken breast, diced into small pieces

Spices (try a mix and match of garlic, lemon peel, pepper, coriander, cardamom, or cinnamon)

Combine all ingredients in a large saucepan along with 2 cups of water and bring to a boil.

Lower the heat and simmer for 20 to 30 minutes. Check on the level of the water and add more as needed. The mix will be done when the sweet potato is fork tender, the lentils have "melted," and the chicken is white. Mash or puree as needed for your baby's texture preferences.

Makes approximately 2 cups.

Freezes with mixed results.

Did You Know?
In addition to being grown in India, the Middle East, and South Asia lentils are grown in the northwestern region of the United States in Washington and Idaho. Most of the lentils grown in the United States are exported to India and China or are used as feed for livestock.

Quick Tip: Lentils can be made either "al dente" or very mushy and "melted." It's up to you how you like them!

Dirty Rice

Tools: sharp knife, medium-sized frying pan, large saucepan

1 pound ground turkey, or a mix of ½ pound ground turkey and ½ pound ground beef

2 tablespoons unsalted butter or olive oil

½ cup each diced onions, red peppers, and celery (aka the trinity)

1½ cups uncooked rice (try basmati, jasmine, parboiled, or white)

Creole spice blend to taste

3 tablespoons minced garlic

3 cups water (I prefer using a mix of 1½ cups chicken stock and 1½ cups water)

Brown the meat in a medium-sized frying pan and drain off excess fat; set aside. Rinse the pan, then heat the butter the same pan and sauté the onions, peppers, and celery until tender; set aside. In a large saucepan, place the rice, spices, garlic, and water (or broth mix), stir, and bring to a boil. Add browned meat and sautéed vegetables to the saucepan and return to a boil. Lower the heat and simmer for 25 to 30 minutes or until the rice is fully cooked. Serve warm.

Freezes well.

Did You Know?
The recipe name Dirty Rice came about because authentic Creole recipes use chicken giblets and livers, which makes the rice dish look dirty. Don't worry, though—even if you're not using giblets and livers, this recipe will still look dirty and your kids might just eat it because it's called "dirty" rice!

Quick Tip: While the traditional southern dirty rice is made with a blend of Creole spices, you may not want to overwhelm baby's palate. Using a blend of milder herbs and spices is just fine; try sage, thyme, garlic, basil, and onion.

This recipe serves 4 to 6 adults.

Beefy Hash Dinner

Tools: vegetable peeler, sharp knife, large frying pan or
skillet with lid, fork, blender or food processor (optional)

    3 large potatoes (any variety but Russet), peeled and
        diced
    ¾ pound thinly sliced stew beef cubes, or ½ pound ground
        beef
    1 medium onion, finely diced
    1 cup beef or vegetable broth (homemade or low-sodium/
        low-fat)
    Pepper to taste

In a large frying pan warmed over medium heat,
combine the potatoes, beef cubes, onion, and beef broth;
add pepper to taste. Cover and simmer until potatoes
are soft enough to mash, the beef is fully cooked, and
the liquid is almost gone, approximately 25 minutes
(add more liquid as needed). Mix well and serve either
mashed, pureed a bit, or as finger food.

Note: If you are using ground beef, brown it in the
frying pan, drain any excess grease, and then add the
potatoes, onion, and beef broth.

Does not freeze well.

Did You Know?
*Many babies do not like the
taste of beef, but the addition
of potatoes and broth to this
recipe might be just the thing*

Quick Tip: Swap
white potatoes for sweet
potatoes or add a few
handfuls of frozen peas
and carrots to make an
interesting colorful dish.

to help change your baby's mind. If not, you can substitute vegetable stock in this recipe.

Quinoa Vegetable Pilaf with Lemon

Tools: sharp knife, frying pan

> 3 cups cooked quinoa
> ½ cup peas (fresh or frozen)
> ½ cup diced carrots (fresh or frozen)
> ½ cup diced zucchini
> Squeeze of lemon juice
> 1 cup chicken or vegetable stock

Combine quinoa, peas, carrots, and zucchini in a frying pan with a quick squeeze of lemon juice and turn stovetop to low.

Stir in the stock little by little, then simmer for 15 minutes if using frozen vegetables. If using fresh vegetables, cook until they are fork tender, 20 to 30 minutes. Serve warm as a side or cold as a salad—babies can eat this cold, too!

Freezes with mixed results.

Did You Know?
You can cook quinoa in any flavor stock that you prefer.

> *Quick Tip:* When making a quinoa pilaf, the key is to add chunkier vegetables to balance out the grain.
>   A bonus with chunky vegetables in this recipe: Baby can pinch and pick away happily!

Scalloped Sweet Potatoes

Tools: vegetable peeler, sharp knife, 2½-quart baking dish, saucepan

Olive oil for greasing
8 medium-sized sweet potatoes
5 tablespoons unsalted butter
½ cup all-purpose flour
2 cups water and 1¾ cups chicken broth
2 tablespoons mayonnaise (optional; use plain whole-milk yogurt if desired)
Quick shake of salt
Cinnamon, nutmeg, and ginger (optional)
Sugar (optional)
Maple syrup (optional)

Preheat oven to 325 degrees and grease the baking dish.

Peel and cut the sweet potatoes in uniform slices, then layer inside the baking dish. Set aside.

Melt the butter in a saucepan; stir in the flour until smooth, and gradually add water/broth mixture, mayonnaise, salt, and spices (if desired). Cook and stir, whisking every few minutes, until thick and bubbly, about 15 minutes over medium heat. Pour mixture over potatoes. (For a sweet treat, mix cinnamon and sugar and then sprinkle on, or drizzle with a bit of maple syrup.) Cover and bake for 2 hours or until tender.

Freezes well: Best reheated in the oven or in a toaster oven to maintain texture.

> *Quick Tip:* This tasty variation of scalloped potatoes takes approximately 2 hours to cook; plan ahead and take advantage of the oven by roasting some veggies or baking some fruits as well.

Did You Know?
This turns out very soft and completely yummy. Your baby will easily be able to eat this as finger food, but do be sure to smoosh or cut into manageable bits.

Green & Orange Fritters

Tools: vegetable peeler, grater, sharp knife, large mixing bowl, frying pan, spatula

- 1 medium carrot, peeled and grated
- 1 medium zucchini, grated
- 1 small onion, chopped
- ⅓ cup ricotta cheese or whole milk
- 1 egg
- ½ cup flour (whole-wheat or all-purpose)
- ¼ teaspoon cayenne pepper or black pepper and/or garlic powder
- Olive oil for frying

Mix the vegetables, ricotta cheese, egg, flour, and pepper in a large bowl; blend well. Add 2 tablespoons of olive oil to the frying pan (1 tablespoon if you are using a small pan) and warm over medium heat. Place large spoonfuls of the batter in the heated frying pan, flatten, and cook for 7 minutes or until golden. Turn over and cook the other side for 7 minutes or until golden. Serve with a dollop of Baby's Cucumber Raita (see page 211) or another dip or sauce of your choosing.

Freezes well: Best reheated in the oven or in a toaster oven to maintain texture.

Did You Know?
Vegetable fritters can be served as a side dish or nutritious snack and will also travel well in a lunch box.

> *Quick Tip:* This recipe is very forgiving—you may substitute the vegetables used here for any vegetable that will grate and cook up easily. You could try sweet potato and zucchini, for example.
>
> If you are looking for a thicker and more pancakelike fritter, simply add an extra ¼ cup of flour.

Banana Fingers

Tools: sharp knife, vegetable peeler, large mixing bowl, frying pan

- 2 to 3 bananas (you may also use 2 to 3 apples)
- 2 cups prepared pancake batter (quick mix or your own homemade mix; use buckwheat pancake mix for denser results), seasoned with spices such as cinnamon, nutmeg, and/or ginger to suit your taste
- 1 tablespoon unsalted butter or olive oil for frying

Cut bananas into ¼-inch slices, either making circles or cutting horizontally to create longer "fingers." (If using apples, peel, core, and slice; I use my spinny-apple-peeler-corer thingy to get this job done.) Dip the banana slices into the pancake batter, making sure the slices are thoroughly coated. Melt butter in frying pan, then drop in the fingers and fry until batter begins to bubble and turns a golden brown. Flip over and fry the other side. Serve warm or cold.

Freezes well: Best reheated in the oven or in a toaster oven to maintain texture.

Did You Know?
A hearty buckwheat pancake mix can be used in a variety of ways. Mix in cheese and small dices of chicken or ham; stir in applesauce and cinnamon; add blueberries or just about anything you can think of. The dense texture makes it great for additions.

> *Quick Tip:* This recipe will likely make a mess of your stovetop, so be prepared! You'll forget all about the mess once you taste these little pancake fingers.

Easy Rice Balls Two Ways

Tools: blender or food processor, spoon, large bowl, pastry brush, frying pan

   2 cups cooked rice (ideally you want to use a sticky rice such as short-grain brown, arborio, or sushi)
   ½ cup veggies or fruit of your choice, diced finely or pureed
   ½ cup cooked meat of your choice
   Spices as desired
   Unsalted butter (for #2)

Rice Balls #1—John and Jake's

Puree rice until it achieves an almost pastelike consistency (or until the grains are small if your baby can handle more texture). Add veggies and/or fruit and puree a bit more. Add meat and puree a bit more. Mixture should be a bit pasty but not so thick that it cannot be easily eaten by your baby.

Shape into little balls and serve either heated (see Quick Tip) or as is. You may serve this on a plate and offer a utensil. For spoon practice, place the mixture in a bowl and give baby a spoon to dig in; the food will cling to the spoon.

An example of this simple rice ball: rice, sweet potato, and chicken with a dash of ginger.

Rice Balls #2—Onigiri Shapes

This involves frying the rice balls lightly so the outside becomes crisp.

First shape the mixture into a square or other shape with straight sides. Brush with a bit of butter and fry.

Freezes well.

Did You Know?
Cooked rice is great for babies learning to feed themselves, as it helps the pincher grasp and fine motor skills develop.

Quick Tip: These rice balls are great when they are baked at 325 degrees for 20 minutes. The outside will be slightly crisp and the rice will take on a nutty flavor.

Be sure not to overdo the pureeing of the fruits, vegetables, or meats. The rice must be able to maintain its shape for proper frying.

❧❀❧

Broccoli Cheddar Nuggets

Tools: sharp knife, baking sheet, large mixing bowl

Olive oil for greasing
1 (16-ounce) package frozen broccoli, cooked, or 2 cups fresh,
   steamed, al dente, cooled broccoli, drained, and chopped
1 cup seasoned bread crumbs
1¾ cups real shredded cheddar cheese (not a "processed
   cheese food")
3 large eggs, or 5 egg yolks
Dash of garlic powder
¼ cup finely diced onions (optional)

Preheat oven to 375 degrees. Lightly coat a baking
sheet with olive oil and set aside.

In a large bowl, combine all ingredients and mix well.
Form mixture into nuggets or fun shapes and place on
baking sheet. Bake for 20 to 25 minutes; turn nuggets
over after 15 minutes. Serve warm.

Note: Chop or mash nuggets if your baby isn't able to
handle bigger finger foods. Also, you may add additional
seasonings if you like—a dash of curry powder, pepper,
extra basil, and oregano, for example. And feel free to
substitute a fruit or veggie puree for the eggs.

Freezes well: Best reheated in the oven or in a toaster
oven to maintain texture.

Did You Know?
*Broccoli is a great source of
soluble fiber, which makes
this a wonderful addition*

Quick Tip: Make an extra
batch and freeze for a quick
snack or side for baby and
for grown-ups, too.

to baby food recipes. Soluble fiber helps loosen up the bowels because it changes its form as it passes through the digestive tract.

Sweet Potato Pancakes I

Tools: mixing bowl, spoon, nonstick frying pan or heavy iron skillet, spatula, serving plate

- ½ cup mashed cooked sweet potatoes
- 1 egg, or 2 egg yolks
- ⅓ cup all-purpose flour (or use graham flour for a nice taste)
- Dash of cinnamon
- Dash of ginger
- ½ teaspoon baking powder
- ¼ to ⅓ cup whole milk (or more)
- 2 tablespoons unsalted butter, melted and then cooled
- ½ teaspoon unsalted butter (if frying in skillet)

Place sweet potatoes in a mixing bowl along with the egg. Stir in the flour and spices, then add the baking powder. Add up to ⅓ cup of milk while stirring, then fold in the butter. The mixture should have the consistency of a thick, lumpy sauce and will resemble an "instant" pancake batter.

Spoon the batter into a nonstick frying pan (you may use a heavy iron skillet if you wish; coat the surface with ½ teaspoon melted butter before frying). Fry until bubbles rise to the surface of the pancakes, then flip over and cook another 2 to 3 minutes until golden brown. Remove pancakes from the frying pan to a plate, then spoon more batter into pan, continuing to fry until the entire batch is cooked. (You may set your oven to warm and keep the finished pancakes on a covered plate in the oven until you are ready to eat.) Before serving, you can drizzle the pancakes with real maple syrup, yogurt, or some warm Berries Jubilee (recipe on page 269).

Freezes well.

Did You Know?
Sweet potatoes are an excellent "binder" and can be made into a custard or used in cake recipes, muffins, and even breads.

> *Quick Tip:* Make an extra batch for the freezer and you'll have a quick breakfast or snack anytime.
>
> Mix a dollop of plain whole-milk yogurt with cinnamon and nutmeg as a spread or dip for the pancakes.

Sweet Potato Pancakes II

Tools: vegetable peeler, sharp knife, steamer basket (optional), saucepan, large bowl, potato masher, frying pan, spatula

    1½ pounds (4 or 5 medium) sweet potatoes
    1 cup cooked basmati or jasmine rice
    ¾ cup frozen baby peas
    ¾ cup frozen diced carrots
    ⅓ cup coarse bread crumbs
    Pinch of ground cardamom

1 garlic clove
1 egg, or 2 egg yolks
2 tablespoons olive oil

Peel and dice, then steam (or boil) the sweet potatoes until tender. In a large bowl, mash the sweet potatoes so that they are not lumpy but not thin. Add the rice, frozen vegetables, bread crumbs, cardamom, garlic, and egg to the mashed sweet potatoes and mix well.

Warm the frying pan and add the olive oil. Spoon out the mixture and fry as you would to make breakfast pancakes, cooking until light brown around the edges. Then flip over and cook the other side until golden brown.

Freezes well.

Did You Know?
This recipe is very versatile; you could replace the peas and carrots with spinach or broccoli or even finely shredded meat.

Quick Tip: Serve with applesauce for dipping or plain whole milk yogurt with avocado and garlic powder.

Mom's Baked Mac-n-Cheese, with or without Treasures

Tools: large pot, large bowl, whisk, saucepan, glass baking dish, blender or food processor (optional)

1 (16-ounce) box elbow or tricolor wheel-shaped pasta
1 egg
Homemade cheese sauce (page 241)—whatever amount you like (2 cups makes it soupy)

2 tablespoons unsalted butter
1 cup bread crumbs
"Treasures" (peas, diced ham, broccoli, carrots, etc.)

Preheat the oven to 350 degrees.

Cook pasta in large pot according to package directions, al dente. In a large bowl, whisk 1 egg into the cheese sauce; set aside. Melt butter in a saucepan and add the bread crumbs, stirring until thoroughly coated; remove from heat. Drain pasta and stir into cheese sauce; add "treasures" as desired.

Place mac-n-cheese in a glass baking dish and sprinkle liberally with the buttered bread crumbs. Bake for 20 to 30 minutes until bubbly and the topping is golden brown. Remove from the oven and cool before serving to baby. (Chop in a blender or food processor if needed.)

Freezes with mixed results: Freeze in small portions for a quick meal or snack. Reheat in a saucepan for best results.

Did You Know?
Mac-n-cheese gets a bum rap, thanks mostly to the boxed bright yellow kind from the grocery store and the version calling for that globular orange cheese block. But homemade mac-n-cheese (especially with the addition of veggies and meats) can be a nutritious and wonderful way to get some fat, protein, calcium, and iron into your older baby.

Quick Tip: Mix and match the types of cheeses you use to make this recipe. I sometimes use a combination of sharp cheddar and the blended Mexican cheese available for tacos.

❧❧❧

Baby's Quick Cereal Teethers

Tools: baking sheet, parchment paper, mixing bowl, rolling pin

- 1 cup all-purpose flour plus extra for sprinkling onto rolling surface
- 1 cup commercial infant cereal (plain rice, mixed grain, or oatmeal)
- ½ cup apple juice
- Pinch of cinnamon
- ¼ teaspoon vanilla extract

Preheat the oven to 350 degrees. Line a baking sheet with parchment paper. Place all ingredients in a mixing bowl with ½ cup of water, mix, and knead into a dough. (Don't worry when you see that the dough is unusual looking. This recipe produces a hard, dense cookie that will not rise owing to a lack of leavening ingredients.) Roll dough out onto a floured surface and cut into teether shapes. (You may also roll the dough into logs and then flatten.) Place teethers onto baking sheet and bake for 25 to 30 minutes until hard. Store in an airtight container.

Makes approximately 12 to 18 cookies, depending on the size and shape you cut out.

Freezes well.

Did You Know?
Commercial baby cereal is great to have on hand for adding to homemade baby food recipes. It may be used to thicken foods that might be too thin and also may be used in cookie, meat loaf, and meatball recipes.

Quick Tip: For added taste, you may use a commercial baby cereal that is flavored, such as banana.

Watch your baby when she is enjoying any type of teething biscuit. Cookie crumbling or breaking may occur, and can be a choking hazard!

***

Graham Cracker Cookies

Tools: 2 large mixing bowls, fork, hand mixer (optional), wooden spoon, rolling pin, sharp knife, cookie sheet

- 2 cups whole-wheat flour and 1 cup all-purpose or graham flour
- 1 teaspoon baking powder
- ½ teaspoon baking soda
- 1 teaspoon cinnamon and/or nutmeg
- ½ cup whole milk
- ⅓ cup maple syrup
- ½ cup unsalted butter, room temperature
- 2 teaspoons vanilla extract
- ½ cup brown sugar

In a medium-sized bowl, mix the flour, baking powder, baking soda, and spices. In another bowl, blend the milk, maple syrup, butter, vanilla, and brown sugar and cream until light and fluffy. Add the wet to the dry ingredients and work in slowly; you may want to use your clean hands for this. Make a big ball with the dough, then knead it a bit. Chill it for 30 minutes, or overnight if you want to wait to bake.

Roll the dough into a thin layer and cut squares. Place

the squares on a large ungreased cookie sheet. (You can also roll out large rectangles and then, using a knife, make deep lines and boxes and prick the squares with the tines of a fork.) Bake at 300 degrees for 25 to 30 minutes until cookies are crisp.

Makes approximately 3 dozen cookies, depending on how you cut the dough.

Freezes with mixed results: Dough will freeze well, but the cookies may not.

Did You Know?
Homemade graham cracker cookies are a healthy alternative to the store-bought variety, and they are so easy to make. A great snack for kids is applesauce on graham crackers with sprinkles of cheddar cheese. This also makes a great snack for older babies who can have all the ingredients and handle the texture. One of the great things about this snack is that the applesauce will soften the cookie a bit.

Quick Tip: Important! There is no way to guarantee that any recipe for homemade teething biscuits or cookies will not crumble or break off into large chunks; even store-bought teethers have been known to break into large chunks and crumble into large bits. Please watch your baby closely and make sure he is sitting up when he is eating biscuits.

Meal in a Muffin

Tools: muffin pan, muffin pan liners (optional), mixing
bowl, sharp knife

  Unsalted butter for greasing
  1½ cups white wheat flour (you may use all-purpose)
  Pinch of salt
  Pinch of apple pie spice
  1 tablespoon baking powder
  2 eggs
  ½ cup milk (or rice or soy milk if preferred)
  ½ cup vegetable oil
  1 cup finely diced (not too small) ham
  1 cup grated sharp cheddar cheese

Preheat oven to 400 degrees. Grease muffin pan or
insert muffin liners. (Liners make for easier cleaning and
better portability.)

Combine flour, salt, apple pie spice, and baking powder
in a mixing bowl. Add the eggs, milk, and oil and mix
well. Fold in the ham and cheese. Fill muffin cups up
to the top (the muffins will not rise very high). Bake at
400 degrees for 20 to 25 minutes or until golden or an
inserted toothpick comes out clean.

Freezes with mixed results.

Did You Know?
*The batter for this muffin recipe is able to incorporate many
different foods. Here are a few variations to replace or
supplement the ham and cheese:*

Broccoli, Chicken, and Cheese

½ cup finely diced or shredded chicken
½ cup chopped (precooked) broccoli
½ cup shredded sharp cheddar
Spices such as onion or garlic powder and sage

Apples, Chicken, and Cheese

½ cup finely diced or shredded chicken
½ cup finely diced apples
½ cup shredded sharp cheddar cheese

Quick Tip: Who doesn't love a muffin? Now, we usually think of muffins as sweet and fluffy, with lots of ooey gooey fruits and sweet toppings. Well, those are the kinds of muffins that I enjoy, anyway.

Skip the fruity ooey gooey and make muffins into a "meal" for your little finger food aficionado. These muffins are portable and will travel to playdates or to day care.

Apple Cheddar Tortilla

Tools: cookie sheet or glass plate

¼ cup applesauce or thinly sliced apples
1 large whole-wheat or plain flour tortilla
½ cup shredded cheddar cheese

Spread the applesauce over the tortilla and sprinkle on the cheddar. Bake on a cookie sheet in a warm oven until the cheese has melted. (You may also warm in the microwave, on a glass plate, at 25-second intervals until the cheese is melted.) Once the cheese is melted, fold the tortilla in half and press the contents throughout so that they fill the tortilla. Allow to cool a bit and then serve straight up!

Does not freeze well.

Did You Know?
Tortillas are now found in white flour, corn, and whole-wheat flour versions. Whenever you are buying tortillas for your baby, get the whole-wheat version for better nutrition!

> *Quick Tip:* Be sure to watch your baby, as my kiddos have been known to try to stuff the whole tortilla into their mouths—even at seven years old!

Avocado Cottage Cheese and Chive

Tools: sharp knife, fork, mixing bowl

1 avocado
1 cup 4% cottage cheese
½ strand of chive, finely chopped

Peel, pit, and mash the avocado. Blend in the cottage cheese and chive, and serve separately or as a spread. This can also be mixed into rice or pasta.

Does not freeze well.

Did You Know?
Cottage cheese is a great transition food; it's just a bit chunky but can be

> *Quick Tip:* Serve this mix within a day or two to prevent browning.

mashed down, and it mixes well with any fruit or veggie you choose.

Sautéed Spinach with Apples and Onions

Tools: frying pan, fork, blender or food processor

- 1 to 2 tablespoons olive oil
- ¼ cup finely chopped onions
- 1 small apple (Macintosh or Granny Smith), peeled, cored, and chopped
- 1 pound spinach, fresh or frozen and thawed

Warm the frying pan and add the olive oil. Add onion and sauté until translucent. Add the apples and sauté until soft. Add the spinach and continue to sauté until spinach is wilting. Allow to cool, then transfer to a blender or food processor to chop or blend as needed for your baby.

Makes approximately 3 servings.

Freezes with mixed results.

Did You Know?
Spinach is a good source of calcium, but it's not fully absorbed because of the oxalates that spinach contains. Spinach will offer you vitamin K as well as vitamin A and folate. Combine with apples for a bountiful source of important nutrients. It seems Popeye knew he was eating a wonderful food to maintain good health!

> *Quick Tip:* Make it a sauce! Allow this to cool and then puree into a sauce; serve over vegetables, pasta, or meats.

Maggie's Mexican Rice

Tools: large saucepan with lid, large spoon, fork

2 tablespoons unsalted butter
1 cup uncooked long-grain brown rice
Cumin, garlic powder, and pepper to taste
Pinch of smoked paprika
½ cup chopped onion
½ can tomato paste mixed with ⅓ cup water, or 2 fresh
  tomatoes, chopped and diced
2 cups low-sodium natural chicken or vegetable broth

In a large saucepan on medium-high heat, melt the butter, then add the rice. Cook, stirring constantly, until the rice becomes golden/translucent. Add the cumin, garlic powder, pepper, and smoked paprika (use your judgment on the amount to add for baby). Now add the onions and cook them until they are translucent and soft. Add the tomato paste and the broth. Allow the ingredients to come to a boil, then turn down the heat to low. Cover the saucepan and simmer for 25 to 30 minutes. Peek in about halfway through and give a stir to prevent possible sticking. Remove from stovetop and allow the saucepan to sit for 5 minutes, then fluff contents with a fork.

Makes approximately 6 adult servings.

Freezes with mixed results.

Did You Know?
This Mexican rice dish is brimming with vitamin A, vitamin C, and iron,

Quick Tip: Be sure not to burn the rice as you are sautéing it prior to adding the other ingredients. Rice can toast up and burn rather quickly.

too. Add some cooked shredded chicken to the rice and you have a tasty and nutritious meal!

✻❀✻

Tofu Nuggets

Tools: sharp knife, plate, shallow mixing bowl, small dish, nonstick baking sheet

- 1 package or block firm tofu (16 ounces)
- ¼ cup all-purpose flour (more might be needed)
- 2 egg yolks
- 1 cup fine dry bread or cracker crumbs (or make a mix of ½ cup each)
- ¼ cup grated Parmesan cheese
- 1 teaspoon garlic powder
- 1 teaspoon onion powder
- Pinch of pepper
- Pinch of curry powder (optional)

Preheat oven to 350°.

Cut tofu into long strips or into your favorite shapes (my kids prefer longer "fingers") and spread flour on a plate. Beat egg yolks in a shallow mixing bowl. Using a separate dish, combine the remaining ingredients.

Coat each piece of tofu in the flour to cover, then dip the tofu into the egg, then dip in the bread crumbs mixture, and place on the baking sheet. Bake for 15 to 20 minutes until crisp.

Allow to cool and serve with a dipping sauce such as pureed sweet potato or pureed peaches from stage one or Appley Yogurt Dip or Baby's Cucumber Raita on pages 214 and 211.

Freezes well: Reheat in a toaster oven or regular oven to maintain texture.

Did You Know?
Current research is conflicting and inconclusive with respect to the pros and cons of eating soy. What we do know is that tofu is packed with calcium, iron, and protein and makes a great finger food for babies.

> *Quick Tip:* Tofu may be stored in the fridge for up to seven days. You must store it in an airtight container of water. The water should be changed daily or at least every two days.

My Favorite Sweet Potato Custard

Tools: medium-sized mixing bowl, casserole dish (1-quart minimum), knife

- 1 cup mashed cooked sweet potato (1 or 2 medium sweet potatos)
- ½ cup mashed banana (about 2 small bananas)
- 1 cup low-fat evaporated milk or low-fat milk
- 2 tablespoons packed brown sugar
- 2 egg yolks, beaten
- ½ teaspoon salt
- ¼ cup raisins or finely chopped figs or dates (optional)
- 1 teaspoon cinnamon and/or nutmeg and/or ginger
- Splash of vanilla extract
- Nonstick cooking spray, as needed

Preheat oven to 325 degrees.

In a medium-sized bowl, mix the sweet potato and the banana, then add the milk; blend well. Add the brown

sugar, egg yolks, salt, raisins (if desired), spices, and
vanilla, and mix thoroughly. Grease the casserole dish
with nonstick cooking spray and add the sweet potato
custard mixture. Bake for 40 to 45 minutes or until a
knife inserted in the center comes out clean.

Allow to cool and then serve. Drizzle with plain whole-
milk yogurt and a bit of maple syrup if desired.

Freezes with mixed results.

Did You Know?
*Custard is much loved by babies and adults alike. This
custard has the added benefit of using supernutritious
sweet potatoes and is packed with protein and all the
vitamins and minerals (including iron) that come from the
egg yolks. Give it a try yourself! This recipe has been in my
(tattered and messy) recipe book for at least fifteen years.
It's so worn that I can barely read the words, but each time I
make it, I think of my older son, who loved to eat it when he
was young. Sadly, he's too cool for custard now!*

Quick Tip: When you are using salt in a baked recipe,
remember that the salt is being spread throughout the
whole recipe; your little one will not be consuming a whole
teaspoon of salt in a tiny piece of baked muffin.

While it is often required in a small amount for a baked
recipe, salt should not be used as a seasoning, nor should
it be used as an addition to flavor the cooked foods your
baby will be eating. Avoid adding salt to everyday foods
for the whole family whenever possible.

Apple Berry Plum Sauce

Tools: vegetable peeler, sharp knife, medium-sized saucepan, potato masher

- 2 apples, peeled, cored, and diced
- 2 handfuls fresh or frozen blueberries
- 2 plums, peeled, pitted, and diced (leave the peel on if baby does not have texture issues)
- 1 teaspoon vanilla extract

Add all fruits and 1 cup of water to a medium-sized saucepan and bring the mixture to a boil over medium-high heat. Lower the heat and simmer for approximately 20 minutes or until fruit is soft and tender; check frequently so you don't run out of water. Cool the mixture, then puree or mash with a potato masher and serve.

Freezes with mixed results.

Did You Know?
This is another super antioxidant, high in vitamin C, tasty, and ready to serve alone or mixed into other foods. You may spoon this over frozen yogurt or cheesecake after you have let your kids have some.

Quick Tip: If you are likely to forget about checking the water level, or you get caught up in playing with your little one, try setting a timer for 5-to-10-minute intervals. The timer will remind you to check the water level and you may be spared from having smoking and burned pots and pans!

Berries Jubilee

Tools: blender or food processor

Use frozen, without sugar or syrup, if fresh berries are
    unavailable:
Cherries, pitted
Strawberries, tops cut off
Blueberries
Raspberries

Combine 1 handful of each berry type and blend until
a sauce texture is achieved. Spoon berries over yogurt,
cereal, sweet potatoes, chicken, or even pork.

Makes approximately 3 cups.

Freezes well.

Did You Know?
*Berries of all types freeze well whole, so having them all
year is not a problem.*

> *Quick Tip:* No need to stew these berries, but if you do,
> save the juice and freeze to add to other foods like cereals,
> yogurts, and meats! To stew the berries, toss them all in
> a saucepan with a small amount of water and simmer for
> 10 minutes.

Roasted Carrots with Fennel

Tools: sharp knife, vegetable peeler, baking dish or
roasting pan, tinfoil

1 bunch carrots (about 5 or 6)
1 fennel bulb
Olive oil for greasing

Preheat oven to 350 degrees.

Trim, peel, and cut carrots into chunks. Cut the stalks off the fennel down to the bulb, then trim off the top and bottom of the bulb. (Save the stalks and add them to a homemade broth, soup, or stock recipe.) Remove the center core area of the fennel bulb and chop fennel into large chunks or dices. Lightly oil a medium-sized baking dish or roasting pan and add the carrots and fennel. Give them a quick mix and pop them into the oven. Bake for approximately 20 minutes, then remove and cover with tinfoil. Pop the pan back into the oven and bake for another 20 minutes or so. Carrots and fennel are cooked when they are fork tender and the fennel has become a little translucent.

You can serve this warm as a side dish or mash it a bit for babies who like texture and self-feeding. If you want to puree it, please let it cool for 10 minutes first. Add water to make it thinner or even use a vegetable or chicken broth.

Freezes well.

Did You Know?
Fennel tastes like a cross between licorice and cabbage. When you roast fennel, it brings out the licorice flavor but adds a slightly nutty twist. It is also a great addition to a roasted potato dish.

Quick Tip: Puree this recipe and add it to your favorite chicken soup, or make it a soup by pureeing and adding to 3 cups of chicken broth with 1 tablespoon flour.

White Potato Treasure Hunt

Tools: vegetable peeler, sharp knife, saucepan, colander, potato masher, handheld blender (optional)

> 5 white potatoes (any variety you wish)
> Unsalted butter (optional)
> Herbs and spices (all optional: rosemary, oregano, garlic powder, dill)
> ½ cup soft-cooked diced vegetables (your choice)

Peel and dice the potatoes. Place the potatoes in the saucepan and cover generously with water. Bring the potatoes to a boil, then lower the heat to medium-high and cook for 20 to 25 minutes or until fork tender.

When the potatoes are cooked, drain the water and return the potatoes to the saucepan. Mash the potatoes with a masher (or whip with a handheld blender). You can add a bit of butter and some herbs and spices if desired.

Take a portion of the mashed potatoes and fill baby's bowl halfway. Add soft-cooked diced vegetables such as peas, carrots, green beans, broccoli, asparagus, beets, or turnip, fold into the potatoes, and serve.

Does not freeze well.

Did You Know?
Potatoes can be divided into two categories, baking and boiling. Baking potatoes are higher in starch and will mash up fluffy and light, whereas boiling potatoes are lower in starch. It may seem counterintuitive, but boiling potatoes are not a good choice for mashing or whipping: they tend

to become lumpy and pasty. Boiling potatoes are called round, white, yellow, and red and are good for potato salads, soups, and other dishes that require a firm potato presence. Baking potatoes, such as russet or Idaho, are great for mashing, French fries, and—you guessed it—baking!

> *Quick Tip:* White potatoes make the perfect backdrop for colored vegetables. When your baby seems to tire of eating solids (and unfortunately this will happen to 99.9 percent of us), send her on a treasure hunt!
>
> Be sure to make enough potatoes for the whole family as a side dish!

Pink Potatoes

Tools: vegetable peeler, sharp knife, 2 large saucepans, potato masher, blender or food processor (optional)

    4 medium-sized white potatoes, peeled and diced
    4 small beets, peeled and diced

Place diced potatoes in a saucepan with enough water just to cover. Bring to a rolling boil and cook over medium-high heat for approximately 20 minutes or until potatoes are fork tender. In another saucepan, add diced beets and enough water to cover. Bring to a rolling boil and cook over medium-high heat for approximately 20 minutes or until beets are fork tender. Once the vegetables have cooked, drain both saucepans and set aside to cool.

Take equal portions of potato and beets and mash or puree together as your baby's texture needs require. Or puree separately and then make a pretty purple dish by swirling white potatoes into a dish of pureed beets. Save the leftovers for dinner or freeze for another day!

Freezes well mashed.

Did You Know?
This colorful mash will be a visual delight as well as a treat for baby's taste buds.

Quick Tip: Beets will stain everything, so be careful when preparing them and letting your baby eat them. If you're going to let baby self-feed, be sure to have a warm, soapy cloth handy to wipe his pink hands and face once he's done. This is truly one of those times where you might want to strip your baby down to eat!

Vegetable or Fruit Meatballs for Baby

Tools: large mixing bowl, large baking sheet, tinfoil

- 1 pound ground turkey, beef, pork, or chicken (you can also use a mix of meats—½ pork and ½ turkey or ½ chicken and ½ beef, for example)
- ¾ to 1 cup bread crumbs
- ¼ cup wheat germ or oat bran
- 1 to 2 cups pureed veggies or fruits (apples, sweet potatoes, pears, spinach, cranberry, broccoli, etc.)
- Spices as desired

Preheat oven to 400 degrees.

Place the ground meat of your choice into a large mixing bowl. Add bread crumbs and wheat germ (you may use oat bran if your baby has wheat allergies/celiac issues). Add veggies and/or fruit to moisten the mixture, ¼ cup at a time. You will have to eyeball the amount of puree added; you are looking to moisten the mix but not make it soupy. Add any spices, if desired.

Mix everything together with your hands (be sure to clean them well or use plastic gloves) until all ingredients are fully combined. Form the mixture into small balls or other shapes of your choosing. Place on a baking sheet and bake at 400 degrees until brown and cooked thoroughly. Cover with tinfoil; be sure not to burn the meatballs, as they will become tough on the outside and baby may not be able to eat them.

Freezes well.

Did You Know?
If you have any purees left in your freezer that you

> *Quick Tip:* Double this recipe to make enough for a family meat loaf!

want to use up, try adding them to this meatball recipe. The purees will act as a binder and you won't need to use eggs; of course, you may add an egg if you want to. You may also use instant baby cereal as a substitute for the wheat germ.

Creamy Tropical Tango

Tools: sharp knife, potato masher, large bowl, blender or food processor (optional)

    ½ cup mashed mango
    ½ ripe banana, peeled and mashed

1 ripe peach, pitted and mashed (remove skin)
Splash of pineapple juice
1 cup plain whole-milk yogurt

Place fruits and splash of juice in a large bowl and mash together. Fold in yogurt until thoroughly combined. Serve as is or mix into baby's cereal or other grain. (To make a smoothie, or if your baby prefers a thin consistency, puree in a blender or food processor.)

Freezes well.

Did You Know?
Mangoes are low in fat and calories but very high in fiber. You will also find lots of vitamins C and B in mangoes as well as iron, potassium, and protein.

> *Quick Tip:* If you are staying away from acidic fruits, omit the pineapple juice and use a splash of pear juice instead.

Apple Turkey Loaf or Sticks

Tools: large mixing bowl, baking sheet or 9 × 5-inch loaf pan, knife, tinfoil (optional)

1 pound ground turkey
1 whole egg, or 2 egg yolks, beaten
½ cup pureed carrots
¼ cup unsweetened applesauce
¼ cup unprocessed natural wheat or oat bran
¼ cup bread crumbs
Pinch of basil
Pinch of garlic powder
Olive oil for greasing

Preheat oven to 350 degrees.

Place ground turkey in a large mixing bowl. Add the egg, carrots, applesauce, bran, bread crumbs, basil, and garlic powder; mix well. (If the mixture appears too dry, add more carrots or applesauce. If it appears too wet, add more bran and/or bread crumbs.)

To make a loaf, lightly oil a loaf pan, spoon in the mixture, and bake at 350 degrees for approximately 45 minutes or until an inserted knife comes out clean. (You may wish to cover with tinfoil to prevent the top from burning.)

Let cool, then remove loaf from pan and slice as you would bread. Break into small bits for finger feeding or mash or chop gently.

Note: This recipe may also be made into "Turkey Sticks" for toddlers and older babies who are able to handle more textured/chunky finger foods. To make sticks, spread the oil on a baking sheet. Divide the mixture evenly, roll it into sticks between the palms of your hands, and place the sticks on the baking sheet. Continue baking as above.

Freezes well.

Did You Know?
Ground beef can easily be used to replace ground turkey in this recipe, and you can pick and choose the fruits and/or vegetables that you wish to use. Let the whole family give this healthy, yummy recipe a try.

Quick Tip: If you wish to bake this in stick form, turn them over halfway through the baking time for uniform texture and cooking.

Smoothies

Tools: blender, various and sundry kitchen tools for food prep

Combine all ingredients in a blender and whizz to a smooth, drinkable texture. Alternatively, whizz just a bit and then serve in a bowl—but get the dropcloth and towels ready!

Autumn Smoothie

½ cup plain, vanilla, or banana whole-milk yogurt
½ cup whole milk
¼ cup canned pumpkin (not the pumpkin pie mix)
¼ cup unsweetened applesauce
1 frozen banana
½ teaspoon cinnamon
¼ teaspoon nutmeg
Dash of ginger

Freezes with mixed results. Serve as a frozen treat if desired.

> *Quick Tip:* Smoothies are nutritious, delicious, and great for sippy cup practice! You can even freeze smoothies into healthy Popsicles.

Banana-Pumpkin Smoothie

1 cup whole milk or whole-milk yogurt
2 tablespoons canned pumpkin (*not* pumpkin pie mix) or homemade pumpkin puree
1 banana

Freezes with mixed results: Do not freeze if using mik. If using yogurt, you can serve as a frozen treat if desired.

Quick Tip: Instead of blending this into a smoothie, mix and serve it as a snack!

Drink Your Greens Smoothie

- 1 cup cleansed fresh kale or spinach
- 1 banana
- 2 fresh pears, cored and diced
- ½ cup fresh strawberries
- ½ cup pineapple or apple juice
- 1 cup ice cubes

Freezes with mixed results: May thaw to an odd texture.

Quick Tip: Using fresh greens in a smoothie will yield a beautiful green hue that is bursting with nutrition and is great eye candy, too!

Strawberry Sunrise Smoothie

- 1 cup fresh strawberries
- 1 banana
- 1 cup plain whole-milk yogurt
- 1 cup cubed mango
- ½ cup plain whole milk (rice or soy milk is fine to use)

Freezes with mixed results: Serve as a frozen treat if desired.

Did You Know?

Making smoothies and healthy juices are just two ways to pack in vitamins C and A. Blending milk-based smoothies adds extra calcium and protein.

Quick Tip: Don't leave this smoothie hanging out on the counter. The bananas will oxidize quickly and the smoothie will change to an unappealing color (the color change isn't harmful, however).

MEALS FOR THE FAMILY—MEALS FOR THE BABY

Feeding your baby homemade meals does not require you to turn yourself into a short-order cook. These quick and easy ideas for the whole family offer well-balanced dinners that your baby may enjoy, too! As a bonus, these recipes give you at least three different meals for your little one that you can puree and freeze using the methods outlined earlier in this book.

These meals will be easy for a stage three eater, but for babies younger than eight months, you may want to serve each food item separately rather than together in one meal. As always, use your judgment and pediatrician's advice to determine if your baby is ready to eat any of the foods shown.

Roast Chicken with Carrots, Parsnips, and Onions

Tools: vegetable peeler, sharp knife, deep roasting pan with lid, turkey baster

    1 whole cut-up chicken (trim fat from the thighs)
    3 medium carrots, peeled and diced
    1 bag of parsnips (about 6 parsnips), peeled and diced
    1 large Vidalia onion, peeled and cut however you prefer
    2 stalks celery, diced
    Thyme, oregano, sage, garlic, pepper, paprika (shake on per
        your taste preferences)

Preheat oven to 375 degrees.
Place chicken in a deep roasting pan, then add the

veggies. Pour 1 cup of water over it all and then shake on the spices.

Cover and roast at 375 degrees for approximately 1½ hours. At the last half hour, remove the lid and let the chicken brown and crisp up.

Check a few times and stir veggies around so they don't stick and burn to the sides of pan; use a turkey baster to gather the juices and then squirt over the chicken and veggies.

Serve with rice pilaf or quinoa and peas.

For Baby (six to eight months old)

Plain Chicken Puree (or shred chicken and freeze in portions)
Carrot Puree
Parsnip Puree
Carrot and Parsnip Puree
Chicken and Carrot Puree
Chicken and Parsnip Puree
Chicken, Parsnip, and Carrot Puree

Salmon with Cranberry Couscous and Asparagus

Tools: small bowl, whisk, shallow baking dish with lid, second baking dish, saucepan, shallow saucepan or baking sheet and tinfoil

⅔ cup maple syrup
1 teaspoon tamari soy sauce
Pinch of ginger, garlic, pepper

1 (1-pound) salmon filet (leave skin on one side, then trim
   when cooked)
Olive oil for greasing
Israeli couscous, packaged or bulk, enough to make 4 servings
½ cup dried cranberries, washed, or ½ cup dried cranberries
1 to 2 pounds asparagus, washed and "snapped" (see
   page 198)

In a small bowl, place maple syrup, tamari, ginger,
garlic, and pepper, then whisk to combine. Position
salmon filet in a shallow baking dish and pour the
maple syrup mixture over it, then cover and marinate in
the refrigerator for 30 minutes (turn the filet over after
15 minutes and continue marinating). Do not marinate
longer than 30 minutes, as fish marinated for extended
time periods will taste funky.

Preheat oven to 450 degrees.

Grease a second baking dish with olive oil and add
the marinated salmon filet. Bake at 450 degrees for
6 minutes per each ½ inch of thickness (1 inch thick
equals 12 minutes of cooking time) or until the salmon
begins to flake.

In a saucepan, prepare couscous according to package
directions, then add the cranberries to the couscous
during the last half of cooking time. In a separate shallow
saucepan, bring 2 cups of water to a rolling boil and then
add the asparagus. Turn off the heat and allow to stand
for 5 to 10 minutes until the asparagus is fork tender.
(You may bake the asparagus if you prefer: Line a baking
sheet with tinfoil, then lay the asparagus down side by
side. Drizzle olive oil over the asparagus, then bake for 10
minutes or until tender.)

For Baby (eight to ten months old)

Plain Salmon Puree (or flake and freeze in portions)
Asparagus Puree
Couscous (make sure cranberries are well mashed down)
Salmon and Asparagus Puree
Asparagus Puree with Added Couscous
Salmon and Couscous Puree

Beef Tenderloin with Roasted Fingerling Potatoes and Green Beans

When you are preparing this for the family, keep in mind that the beef should be cooked well, with no pink or running juices that are not clear. Babies should only be served meats that are fully cooked.

Tools: mixing bowl, small bowl, 2 roasting pans, meat thermometer, sharp knife, tinfoil (as cover, if needed), shallow saucepan

1 beef tenderloin, 3 to 4 pounds
⅓ cup balsamic vinegar
1 clove garlic, crushed
Pepper, garlic powder, pinch of salt to taste
Olive oil for greasing
1 pound fingerling potatoes
1 pound green beans, trimmed in the package and scrubbed
    clean

Place beef in a mixing bowl. Mix vinegar and crushed garlic, then pour over the meat. Combine pepper, garlic powder, and salt in a small bowl, then rub into the meat. Marinate in refrigerator for 1 hour.

Preheat oven to 425 degrees.

Transfer beef to a roasting pan, insert meat thermometer, and place in oven, uncovered, to roast for 20 minutes at 425 degrees.

Wash and scrub fingerling potatoes. Cut in half if desired. Grease a second roasting pan and add fingerlings.

Once beef has roasted for 20 minutes at 425 degrees, lower the temperature to 375 degrees, cover with lid or tinfoil, and roast for an additional 40 minutes or until meat thermometer reads 160 degrees. About 20 minutes into this part of the beef roasting time, place fingerlings into oven and roast alongside the tenderloin.

In a shallow saucepan, bring 1 cup of water to a rolling boil and then add the green beans. Lower heat and simmer for 6 minutes or until fork tender.

When tenderloin is finished cooking, remove from oven and let it rest, covered, for 10 minutes prior to serving.

For Baby (eight to ten months old)

Plain Beef Puree (or shred and freeze in portions)
Green Bean Puree
Fingerling and Green Beans (mashed or chopped, for finger food)
Beef and Green Bean Puree
Green Bean and Fingerling Puree
Fingerling and Beef Puree

Homemade Chicken Pot Pie with Pumpkin Cornbread

This recipe makes a hearty chicken pot pie that the whole family will enjoy. You can serve a piece to your baby if you'd like, but keep in mind the recipe contains dairy and wheat.

Tools: vegetable peeler, sharp knife, saucepan, mesh strainer, whisk, baking sheet, 9-inch pie pan, fork

- 1 pound boneless, skinless chicken breasts, cut and diced into small pieces
- 1 cup peas (frozen or fresh)*
- 1 cup peeled and diced carrots (dice into disks or small chunks; frozen carrots are okay)*
- Sprinkle of thyme, sage
- 5 tablespoons unsalted butter
- ¼ cup finely diced celery
- ¼ cup finely chopped onions
- 1 clove garlic, crushed
- ¼ teaspoon each pepper, rosemary, thyme, sage
- ⅓ cup all-purpose or whole-wheat flour, to be used as thickener
- 2 cups low- or no-sodium chicken broth or stock
- ⅔ cup whole milk
- 2 (9-inch) pie crusts, unbaked

Preheat oven to 425 degrees.

Bring 5 or 6 cups of water to a boil in saucepan, then add the chicken, peas, and carrots. Sprinkle in some thyme and sage and bring to a boil, then lower heat to medium. Continue to boil for 15 minutes or until chicken

---

* Time-saver: Use a 16-ounce bag of frozen mixed peas and carrots.

is fully cooked (will turn white), then drain in mesh strainer and set aside. Rinse out the saucepan and return to stove. Add the butter, celery, onions, garlic, pepper, rosemary, thyme, and sage, and cook on medium heat until the vegetables are translucent and soft. Add the flour and stir to combine and make a roux, then slowly add the broth and milk, whisking constantly. Lower heat and simmer for 15 to 20 minutes until the mixture has thickened.

Prepare the pie pan by laying down the bottom crust, then add the chicken and vegetables. Place the pie pan on a baking sheet to help cook the bottom crust and catch any drips. When the sauce has finished thickening, pour over the pie crust and veggies. Add the top crust (be sure to pinch sides tightly to minimize overflow) and use the tines of a fork to prick the top crust so that steam is released. Bake for 30 to 40 minutes.

For Baby (eight to ten months old)

You may wish to set aside some chicken and vegetables for babies younger than eight months who may not be used to all of the ingredients. Don't worry about the butter used here; babies need fats, and a bit of butter will do no harm. You may even wish to scoop out a bit of the finished mixture and puree or mash it to serve by itself!

Plain Chicken Puree (or shred and freeze in portions)
Pureed Peas
Pureed Carrots
Pureed Peas and Carrots
Pureed Peas, Carrots, and Chicken

Pumpkin Cornbread

Tools: 8-inch square baking pan (round will work),
2 mixing bowls, spatula, toothpick

Oil for greasing
1 cup cornmeal
1 cup whole milk
1 cup flour (I use white wheat flour, King Arthur brand;
    whole-wheat makes a very dense cornbread)
⅓ cup sugar
3 teaspoons baking powder
Pinch of nutmeg, ginger, allspice, cinnamon
1 egg
⅓ cup vegetable oil
¾ cup pumpkin puree, homemade or canned (*not* the
    pie mix)

Preheat oven to 400 degrees. Lightly grease the
baking pan.

Combine the cornmeal and milk in one bowl and let
stand for 15 minutes. In a second bowl, combine the flour,
sugar, baking powder, and spices. When the 15 minutes is
up, transfer contents of the second bowl to the first bowl,
then add the egg, oil, and pumpkin puree. Mix well and
pour into the baking pan. Bake for 20 to 25 minutes or until
a toothpick comes out clean and the bread has risen a bit.

For Baby (eight months)

Crumble a slice into manageable pieces and serve.

Baked Haddock with Garlic Mashed Potatoes, Sautéed Summer Squash

Tools: vegetable peeler, sharp knife, glass baking dish, large saucepan, potato masher, large sauté pan

- 1 pound haddock, cut into 3 or 4 filets
- 3 tablespoons unsalted butter, melted
- 2 cloves garlic, minced
- Dash of pepper, oregano (for fish)
- 1 lemon, sliced in half
- 6 medium-sized Idaho or russet white potatoes, peeled and diced
- Dash of pepper (for potatoes)
- 2 tablespoons olive oil
- 1 pound zucchini, washed and sliced into disks
- 1 pound yellow/crookneck squash, washed and sliced into disks
- 2 basil leaves, chopped, or 2 teaspoons dried basil

Preheat oven to 350 degrees.

Arrange haddock filets in a glass baking dish, then drizzle butter evenly over fish. Sprinkle fish with 1 clove of minced garlic, pepper, and oregano, then squeeze lemon over fish. Transfer to the oven and bake for 20 minutes or until the fish begins to flake.

In a large saucepan, add diced potatoes and enough water to cover them; bring to a boil and cook for approximately 25 minutes or until fork tender. Drain and then mash with remaining clove of garlic and a dash of pepper.

Warm a large sauté pan over medium heat with olive oil, then add the squash. Sauté until tender, adding basil during the last few minutes of sautéing.

For Baby (eight to ten months old)

Pureed Haddock (or serve in flakes)
Mashed Potatoes
Pureed Zucchini
Pureed Yellow Squash
Pureed Haddock and Mashed Potatoes
Pureed Haddock with Squash

APPENDIX I

Freezing Foods Chart

The frozen foods table presented here has been established from personal experience with freezing homemade baby food—a lot of experience, having to feed twins. You may have better, or worse, luck with freezing your homemade baby food cubes.

Freezing Foods

Table accounts for foods that have been cooked and/or pureed raw.

Type of Food	How It Will Freeze When Pureed
FRUITS	Cooked and Raw
Apples	May turn brown (cooked)—freeze in slices for a nice teething reliever (raw)
Apricots	May not freeze solid and texture may be altered (raw or cooked)
Avocados	May turn brown when pureed—best frozen in halves with a bit of lemon juice (raw)
Bananas	May brown when pureed—best to cut in half, wrap, then freeze (raw)

continued

Type of Food	How It Will Freeze When Pureed
FRUITS	Cooked and Raw
Blueberries	Freeze well whole or pureed—may thaw to a watery consistency (raw or cooked)
Cherries	Freeze well whole or pureed—may thaw to a watery consistency (raw or cooked)
Citrus	Does not freeze well
Coconut	Does not freeze well
Cranberries	Freeze well whole or pureed—may thaw to a watery consistency (raw or cooked)
Figs	Unknown
Grapes	Freeze well whole, halved, or quartered (raw)
Kiwi	May be gritty/watery when thawed (raw)
Mangoes	May be gritty/watery when thawed—best frozen in chunks (raw or cooked)
Melons	May be gritty/watery when thawed—best frozen raw in chunks (raw or cooked)
Nectarines	Freeze well, may be gritty/watery when thawed—freeze in chunks (raw or cooked)
Papaya	Freezes well, may be gritty/watery when thawed—freeze in chunks (raw or cooked)
Peaches	Freeze well, may be gritty/watery when thawed—freeze in chunks (raw or cooked)
Pears	May turn brown—freeze well, may be gritty/watery when thawed (raw or cooked)
Persimmons	Unknown
Plums	Freeze well, may be gritty/watery when thawed (raw or cooked)
Prunes	Freeze well, but may not freeze solid and texture may be altered (raw or cooked)
Pumpkin	Freezes well (cooked)
Strawberries, Raspberries, Blackberries	Freeze well whole and raw or simmered into a puree or sauce/syrup

Type of Food	How It Will Freeze When Pureed
VEGETABLES	Cooked
Asparagus	Freezes well, but may be watery when thawed—best frozen in pieces
Beans (Dried/ Lentils)	Freeze well
Beans (Green)	Freeze well, but may be gritty/watery when thawed—best frozen in individual pieces
Beets	Freeze well
Broccoli	Freezes well, but may be watery when thawed—best frozen in pieces
Carrots	Freeze well
Cauliflower	Freezes well, but may be watery when thawed—best frozen in pieces
Corn	Freezes well, but may be watery when thawed—best frozen without being pureed
Cucumber	Does not freeze well
Eggplant	Freezes well, but may be watery when thawed—best frozen without being pureed
Leeks	Mixed results—best frozen within another dish/meal
Onions	Mixed results—best frozen within another dish/meal
Parsnips	Freezes well, but may be gritty/watery when thawed
Peas	Freeze well, but may be gritty/watery when thawed
Peppers	Mixed results—best frozen within another dish/meal
Potato, White	Freezes well, but may be gritty/watery when thawed; lots of reconstituting needed
Spinach	Mixed results
Squash, Winter (Butternut etc.)	Freezes well

continued

Type of Food	How It Will Freeze When Pureed
VEGETABLES	Cooked
Squash, Summer (Zucchini etc.)	Freeze well, but may be very gritty/watery when thawed
Sweet Potato	Freezes well
Tomatoes	Best frozen as a "sauce," may be watery when thawed
Turnip	Freezes well, but may be gritty/watery when thawed
MEATS/ PROTEINS	Cooked
Beef	Mixed results—may be gritty/watery when thawed; freeze in cooked pieces
Chicken	Mixed results—may be gritty/watery when thawed; freeze in cooked pieces
Eggs	Do not freeze well pureed, but will freeze with mixed results when scrambled or fried
Fish	Mixed results—may be gritty/watery when thawed; freeze in cooked pieces
Pork	Mixed results—may be gritty/watery when thawed; freeze in cooked pieces
Tofu	Mixed results—may be very gritty/watery when thawed; freeze in chunks in water
Turkey	Mixed results—may be gritty/watery when thawed; freeze in cooked pieces
GRAINS	Cooked
Barley	Mixed results—may be rubbery or gritty when thawed; best frozen, not pureed
Buckwheat/ Kasha	Mixed results—may be rubbery or gritty when thawed; best frozen, not pureed
Flax	N/A
Kamut	Mixed results—may be rubbery or gritty when thawed; best frozen without being pureed

Type of Food	How It Will Freeze When Pureed
GRAINS	Cooked
Millet	Mixed results—may be rubbery or gritty when thawed; best frozen, not pureed
Oatmeal	Mixed results—may be rubbery or gritty when thawed; best frozen, not pureed
Pasta	Does not freeze well—may be rubbery or gritty when thawed; best frozen whole
Quinoa	Mixed results—may be rubbery or gritty when thawed; best frozen without being pureed
Rice	Mixed results—may be rubbery or gritty when thawed; best frozen without being pureed
DAIRY	Cooked
Cheese	Mixed results—best frozen in chunks, cubes, or shreds; melted and then frozen cheese may thaw to a rubbery texture
Milk	Mixed results—can be frozen, but will separate
Yogurt	Mixed results—may separate when thawed; best frozen and eaten in frozen form or added to other foods (smoothie time!)

Charting Baby's Solid Food Adventures

If there is one thing to be said about charts, it's that you either love them or you hate them. Many parents find it helpful to refer to a chart of foods that are age-appropriate for their infants. The charts on the following pages list foods that are appropriate for each of the three stages, so that you can pick and choose when (and if) you want to serve your baby these foods. The most important thing to remember about any chart is that it is intended to offer suggestions and guidelines for your consideration. Always feed your baby according to your pediatrician's recommendation and your baby's needs and cues and *not* according to any chart.

First Foods for Baby Chart—Four to Six Months Old

The foods listed in this chart are all wonderful starters for babies. They are not known to cause terrible digestive upsets, nor are they highly allergenic.

Foods for Baby

FOUR TO SIX (4-6) MONTHS OLD

CEREALS & GRAINS: Barley, Oat, Rice
FRUITS: Apples, Avocados, Bananas, Pears
VEGETABLES: Acorn/Butternut Squash, Green
    Beans, Sweet Potatoes
PROTEIN: None
DAIRY: None

Second Foods for Baby Chart—Six to Eight
Months Old

Whether your baby is just starting her solid food adventures or is already becoming a fabulous foodie, the foods shown in this chart will expand her palate and bring heaps of joy to her taste buds. Incorporating spices and herbs to baby's food will let you add zip and flavor without having to rely on salt or sugars.

Foods for Baby

SIX TO EIGHT (6-8)
MONTHS OLD

CEREALS & GRAINS: Barley, Oat, Rice
FRUITS: Apples, Apricots, Avocado, Bananas,
    Mangoes, Nectarines, Peaches, Pears, Plums,
    Prunes, Pumpkin
VEGETABLES: Acorn/Butternut Squash, Carrots,
    Green Beans, Parsnips, Peas, Sweet Potatoes,
    Yellow Squash/Zucchini
PROTEIN: Chicken, Tofu, Turkey
DAIRY: Cheese (closer to eight months), Plain
    Whole-Milk Yogurt

It's time to think about experimenting with spices!

Third Foods for Baby Chart—Eight Months and Older

From eight months of age, it's a no-holds-barred food festival.

Foods for Baby

EIGHT MONTHS AND OLDER

GRAINS & SEEDS: Amaranth, Flax, Kamut, Millet, Pasta, Quinoa, Sesame, Spelt, Wheat

FRUITS: Blueberries, Cherries, Citrus, Cranberries, Dates, Figs, Grapes, Kiwi, Melons, Papaya, Pineapple, Raspberries, Strawberries

VEGETABLES: Artichokes, Asparagus, Beets, Broccoli, Cauliflower, Corn, Cucumbers, Eggplant, Leeks, Mushrooms, Onions, Peppers, Spinach, Tomatoes, Turnip, White Potatoes

PROTEIN: Beans/Legumes, Beef, Fish, Ham (natural), Pork, Tofu

DAIRY: Cheddar, Cream Cheese, Cottage Cheese, Colby, Jack (no soft cheeses such as Brie!)

Combined Solid Food Chart

Foods for All Ages

Age	Fruits	Vegetables	Meats and Proteins	Grains	Dairy
4–6 months	Apples Avocados Bananas Pears	Green beans Sweet potato Winter squash (such as butternut)		Barley Oatmeal Rice	
6–8 months	Apricots Mangoes Nectarines Papaya Peaches Plums Prunes Pumpkin	Carrots Parsnips Peas	Chicken Tofu Turkey		Cheese Yogurt
8 months and older	Blueberries Cantaloupe (Melons) Cherries Citrus Coconut Cranberries Figs Grapes Kiwi Persimmons Strawberries	Asparagus Beans (dried/lentils) Beets Broccoli Cauliflower Corn Cucumber Eggplant Leeks Onions Peppers Potato, white Spinach Summer squash (such as zucchini and yellow) Tomatoes Turnips	Beef Eggs Fish Pork	Buckwheat/kasha Flax Kamut Millet Pasta Quinoa	Cheese Cottage cheese Cream cheese
12 months					Cow's milk

Seasonal Fruits and Vegetables

Living in the United States, we are a bit lucky when it comes to the availability of fresh fruits and veggies. It seems that something yummy is always growing in one part of the country or another. Here are just a few fruits and vegetables and the months that you may expect to find them fresh. Be sure to check in your area to see what is locally grown each season. By eating locally, you not only enjoy fresher foods, you also support your local farmers.

Fruit Seasons

Apricots June–July
Avocados December–March
Bananas All year (mostly imported, however)
Cantaloupe May–September
Cherries May–June
Grapes June–December
Honeydew February–October
Kiwis June–August
Mangoes April–August

Nectarines and Peaches June–September
Papayas All year (mostly imported, however)
Plums June–September
Strawberries February–August
Watermelons May–August

Vegetable Seasons

Artichokes March–May
Asparagus March–June
Beets June–October
Cabbage All year
Carrots All year
Corn May–September
Cucumbers May–August
Green or Wax Beans April–October
Lima Beans April–August
Onions All year
Peas, Green April–July
Peppers All year
Spinach March–May
Summer Squash (such as zucchini and yellow squash)
    June–August
Tomatoes May–August
White Potatoes All year
Winter Squash (such as acorn and butternut)
    October–January

APPENDIX IV

References, Resources, and Links

Nutrition and Foods

American Diabetes Association—http://www.diabetes.org

Eat Right.org, from the American Dietetic Association—
http://www.eatright.org

USDA Nutrient Database (searchable database with
information on the nutrients in foods)—
http://www.nal.usda.gov/fnic/foodcomp/search

Food Facts.com (searchable database with information
on the processed and packaged foods we buy)—
http://www.foodfacts.com

USDA Food and Nutrition Information Center—
http://fnic.nal.usda.gov/nal_display/index
.php?info_center=4&tax_level=1

Fruits and Veggies Matter (from the Centers for Disease
Control)—http://www.fruitsandveggiesmatter.gov

For Information on Freezing Foods

Freezing Basics, Clemson University Extension, publication
HGIC 3060

Freezing Prepared Foods, Clemson University Extension,
publication HGIC 3065

Freezing Fruits and Vegetables, Clemson University
Extension, publication HGIC 3063

Food Safety and Inspection Services, USDA, Freezing and
Food Safety Fact Sheet, June 2010 www.fsis.usda.gov/
factsheets/focus_on_freezing/index.asp

Food and Drug Administration, Refrigerator and Freezer
Storage Chart, www.fda.gov/downloads/Food/
ResourcesForYou/HealthEducators/ucm109315.pdf

Food Allergy Information

American Academy of Allergy, Asthma & Immunology—
http://www.aaaai.org

Asthma and Allergy Foundation of America—http://www
.aafa.org

Food Allergy and Anaphylaxis Network—http://www
.foodallergy.org

North American Society for Pediatric Gastroenterology,
Hepatology and Nutrition—http://www.naspghan.org/
sub/Food_Allergy.htm

NIH, Medline Plus: Food Allergy—http://www.nlm.nih
.gov/medlineplus/ency/article/000817.htm

Allergic Child—http://www.allergicchild.com

Dr. Sears—Tracking Down Food Allergies—http://www
.askdrsears.com/html/4/t041800.asp

Allergy Kids—http://www.allergykids.com

All Health Related

American Academy of Pediatrics—http://www.aap.org

AAP Policy Publications search engine—http://aappolicy
.aappublications.org

World Health Organization—http://www.who.int/en

Centers for Disease Control—http://www.cdc.gov

PubMed, from the National Institutes of Health—http://
www.ncbi.nlm.nih.gov/pubmed

Medscape from WebMD—http://www.medscape.com

Pediatrics, the official medical journal of the
American Academy of Pediatrics—http://pediatrics
.aappublications.org

Contemporary Pediatrics—http://www
.contemporarypediatrics.com

Alberta Children's Services—http://www.child.gov.ab.ca

United Nations University. Use search feature for great food
and nutrition publications—http://unu.edu/publications

Pediatricians on the Web

Dr. Greene's Housecalls—http://www.drgreene.com

AskDrSears.com—http://www.askdrsears.com

Dr. Spock—http://drspock.com

Seattle Mama Doc—http://seattlemamadoc
.seattlechildrens.org

INDEX

ABOUT THE AUTHOR

Margaret (Maggie) Meade is the creator of the highly respected and trusted website Wholesome Baby Food.com. For over eight years she has been dedicated to creating a website that inspires and empowers parents to make fresh and delicious real food for their babies. Born in Northampton, Massachusetts and a graduate of Miss Hall's School in Pittsfield, she was taught early on that there were no limits to the places she could go or the things she could do with her talents and knowledge. While attending college in Florida, a devastating car accident altered her life forever. She began to informally study nutrition and developed a passion for healthy cooking, knowing that nurturing foods were important for healing the body and the soul. Maggie is not a professional chef nor has she ever attended culinary school. It is so simple to nurture and feed babies with healthy and nutritious homemade foods: no advanced education required. Currently living in New Hampshire with her husband, three sons, a German shepherd, and a tabby cat, Maggie enjoys cooking, reading, travel, camping with the family, and writing for Wholesome Baby Food.com and Momtastic.com.